OTHER RUSSIAS

Victoria Lomasko

TRANSLATED FROM THE RUSSIAN
BY THOMAS CAMPBELL

n+1 BOOKS

n+1 FOUNDATION   NEW YORK

This book is dedicated to Bela Shayevich and Thomas Campbell

Published 2017 by n+1 Foundation

68 Jay Street, Ste. 405

Brooklyn, New York

www.nplusonemag.com

Special thanks to Deena Butt, Chantal Clarke,
Dilara O'Neil, Bela Shayevich, and Dayna Tortorici

ISBN 978-0-9970318-4-3

Printed by the Sheridan Press

Manufactured in the United States of America

Design by Rachel Ossip

Second Printing

OTHER RUSSIAS

P.S. 1 Symposium: A Practical Avant-Garde

What We Should Have Known: Two Discussions

What Was the Hipster?: A Sociological Investigation

The Trouble is the Banks: Letters to Wall Street

No Regrets: Three Discussions

Buzz: A Play

CONTENTS

INTRODUCTION

This book collects my graphic reportage from 2008 to 2016, years I spent traveling to Russian cities and villages to speak with people who live on the margins of Russian society. Based in drawings produced from life (rather than reproduced from photographs), this work addresses two broad subjects, and thus comprises two sections: "Invisible" and "Angry."

"Invisible" contains stories about juvenile prison wards, teachers and pupils at rural schools, migrant workers, old people seeking refuge in Russian Orthodoxy, sex workers, and single women in the Russian hinterlands. As the majority of the Russian populace is "invisible" to itself and to the rest of the world, this section could be expanded indefinitely. What makes these subjects distinct, however, and distinctly invisible, is their social isolation: they have no way to "move up" in life, and no access to the public arena.

"Angry," meanwhile, chronicles people's attempts to come together and take back their voice and rights from the state. It includes reports of the large opposition rallies that took place in Moscow in 2012 and the subsequent trials of protesters; the LGBT community's efforts to stay visible despite the government's adoption of homophobic laws; and protests by national and local grassroots "pressure groups" in 2015 and 2016.

"Graphic reportage" may strike Western readers as a strange or hybrid genre. While my stories may be read through the prism of European and American nonfiction or documentary comics, they were produced under different circumstances and with a different tradition in mind. After the collapse of the Soviet Union, the official Union of Artists and its obligatory socialist realism were replaced by contemporary art institutions that championed, with equal fervor, socialist realism's supposed opposite: Western conceptualism and an unspoken taboo on realistic figurative art, especially life drawing. In 2007, the Russian art critic Ekaterina Degot wrote, "If an artist wants to do something really scandalous today, something that will get them turned down for an exhibition, they should produce a realist oil painting. Or draw a human figure with pencil on paper."

At the fashionable art school I attended after earning a bachelor's degree in art from a more conventional university, my first work of graphic reportage was rejected out of hand. I was told that no one drew from life in the 21st century. But I felt the need to complete my drawings on the spot, to serve as a conductor for the energy generated by events as they happened. I refused to make drawings from photos and videos.

The usual methods of Western documentary comics were not conducive to what I wanted to do, either, since their frame-by-frame layout felt at odds with the sense of immediacy that I was after. Finding no guides among my contemporaries, I turned to the practices of the 19th and 20th centuries—namely to the albums produced by Russian soldiers, concentration camp inmates, and people who experienced the Nazi siege of Leningrad. In many cases, urgent work like this was the only kind of reporting that was done in these brutal conditons—these albums were the sole acts of witness. In such circumstances, what kind of responsibility does an artist have? What I was trying to do, above all, was to break through to a more direct grasp and reflection of the reality around me.

Pursuing this kind of life drawing was also my way of protesting the insular Russian art scene, and the complete social alienation of artists from viewers—and vice versa. The people from different social groups whose lives I reported on also had scant notion of how other social classes in their own country lived. To present a true picture of Russian society, I found I had to become an independent researcher, journalist, and activist. I made working at the crossroads of journalism and human rights activism my creative method.

The book shows how Russian society has been changed in recent years by pervasive censorship, the passage of new laws controlling virtually all aspects of life, and the utter fusion of the Russian Orthodox Church with the bureaucracy. (Just compare the outsiders in "A Prayer Against the General Plan" with the confident members of the grassroots Orthodox movement Multitude, who appear in the book's final piece, "Truckers, Torfyanka, and Dubki.") On the other hand, discontent and anger have long been growing, engulfing parts of society once indifferent to politics and loyal to the authorities.

Over the years, my approach has changed. In 2008, my only desire was to avoid getting stuck in the sterile white cube of the gallery and get over my fear of reaching out to "ordinary" people. At first, I returned to the practice of sketching in public places but added what my subjects were saying to the drawings. I eavesdropped and spied on them. Then I worked up the courage to engage them in conversation and ask questions. Later, I began to approach my subjects as a journalist would, traveling to various places to research topics that fascinated me.

I hope my graphic reportage from this eight-year period will give readers insights into Russian society and a sense of the changing social and political landscape. I think of what follows as a story of ordinary people, unfolding against the larger background of history.

ЛОМАСКО

"Do you have a priest's blessing to draw us?"

INVISIBLE

BLACK PORTRAITS

I drew each of the following portraits after a chance meeting with a stranger who wanted to tell me about his or her life. Such situations cannot be forced, so this series of eight drawings took shape over three years. For example, the old retired teacher suddenly sat down next to me in a Moscow suburban train. The tattooed young man approached me in a hospital courtyard, while the stonemason, Sergei, came up to me at a protest rally by Russian Orthodox activists. (You will meet Sergei again in the next series, "A Prayer Against the General Plan.") The circumstances in which these people found themselves were painful, so I decided to use a black background for the portraits.

The views and attitudes evinced by the sitters in "Black Portraits" are quite typical of our society. Especially telling is the diptych that emerged between the portraits of Sergei and Viktor, a lecturer in political science. It embodies the prevailing political moods in Russia: the poor and less educated social groups are opposed to "the West," while "the intelligentsia" despises "the common folk."

"The West wants to destroy the bold and beautiful Russian people."

Stonemason Sergei, once a militant atheist, is now an Orthodox activist.

"Russians are shit. But me, I'm seventh-generation intelligentsia."

Viktor Mizin is a lecturer in political science at MGIMO, the Moscow State Institute of International Relations. He was born at Grauerman Maternity Hospital in central Moscow.

"After Dad got hit by a trolleybus, things got quite lonely."

Пошёл к храму с мыслью о том, как бы лучше его взорвать, а вернулся с огромным желанием восстановить его и всю снесённую Москву.

"I went to a church thinking how best to blow it up, but I came back with a great desire to restore it—and everything else that has been demolished in Moscow."

We are sitting in the hall,
The doctor waiting to see.
An artist sits cheek by jowl:
Here is how she drew me.
I had a look at what she's done.
It seems I've changed.
In my heart I thought I was young,
But when I looked, I was amazed.

Fifteen minutes later, Sergei Fyodorovich, a self-described poetaster, would learn that his wife would go blind in one eye.

"I got a call. 'The last old man has died.' Our village no longer exists."

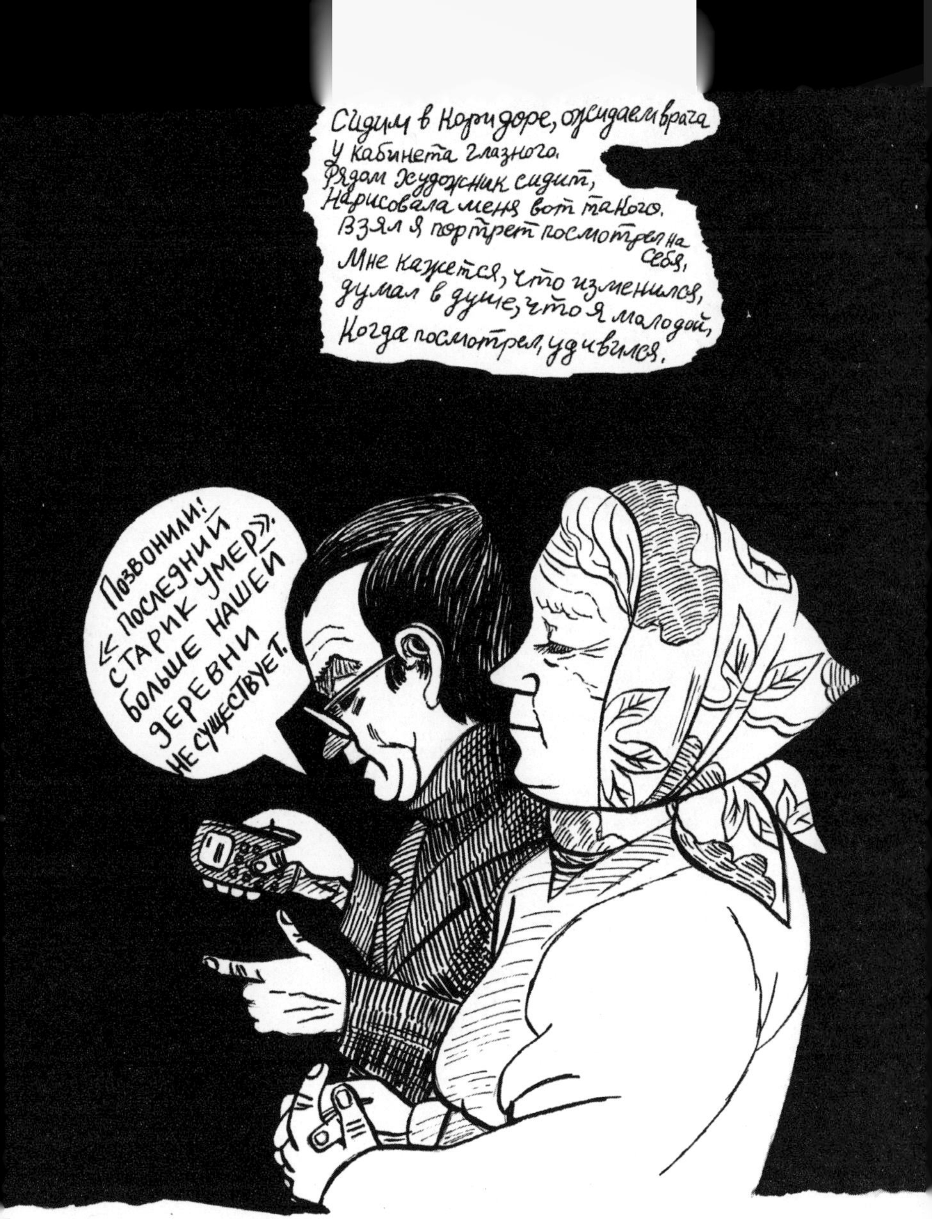
Сидим в Коридоре, ожидаем врача
У кабинета глазного.
Рядом художник сидит,
Нарисовала меня вот такого.
Взял я портрет посмотрел на себя,
Мне кажется, что изменился,
думал в душе, что я малодой,
Когда посмотрел, удивился.
Позвонили! «Последний старик умер». Больше нашей деревни не существует.

A woman recites Alexander Pushkin's "Ode to Liberty" in the subway:

> And silent stands the faithless guard,
> The drawbridge downed without alarm,
> The gate in dark of night unbarred
> By treason's mercenary arm.
> O shame! O terror of our time!
> Those Janissary beasts burst in
> And slash, the Criminal Sovereign
> Is slaughtered by unholy crime.

"Pushkin is our great poet. Everything else is tawdry."

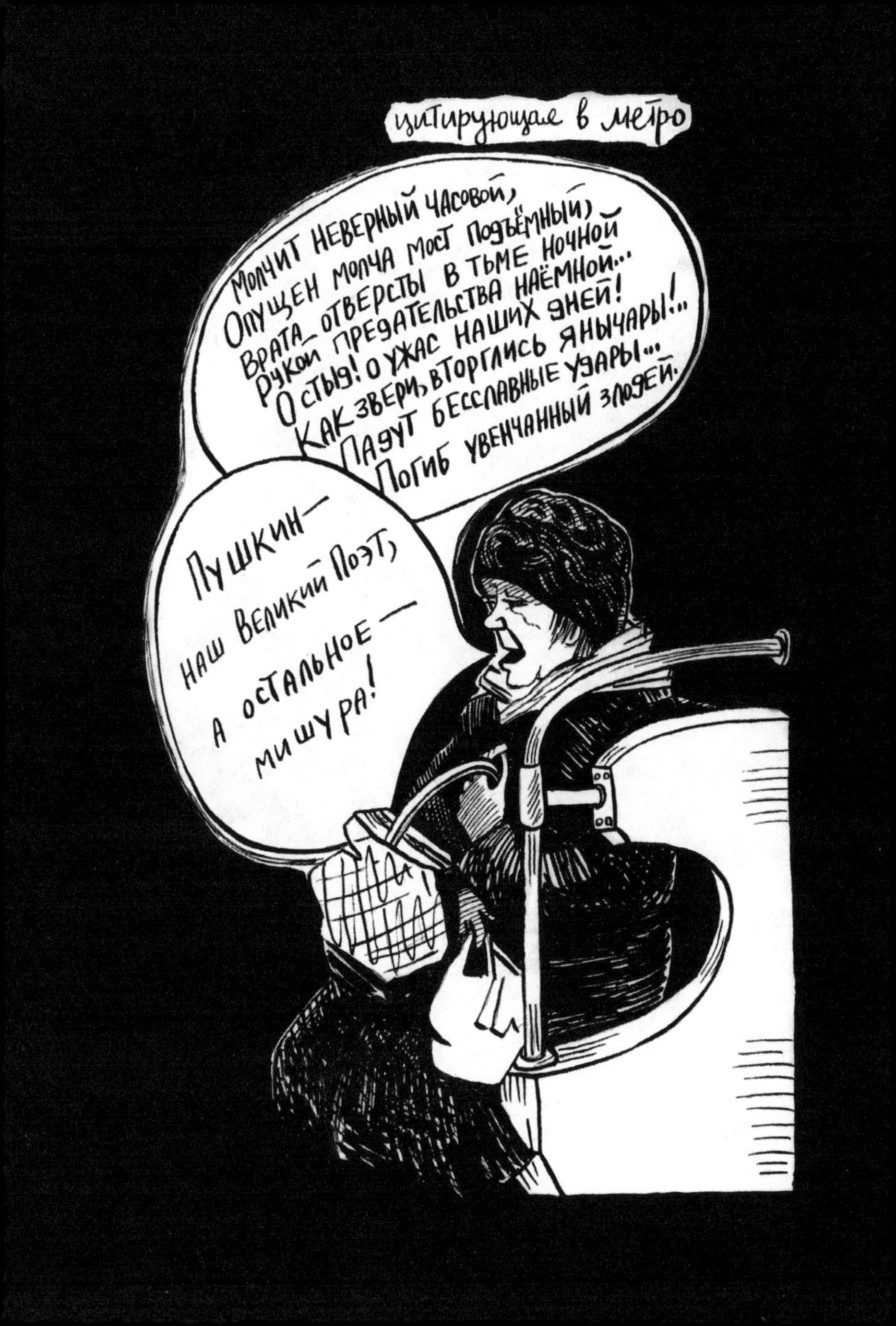
цитирующая в метро
Молчит неверный часовой, Опущен молча мост подъёмный, Врата_отверсты в тьме ночной Рукой предательства наёмной... О стыд! О ужас наших дней! Как звери, вторглись янычары!.. Падут бесславные удары... Погиб увенчанный злодей.
Пушкин— наш Великий Поэт, а остальное— мишура!

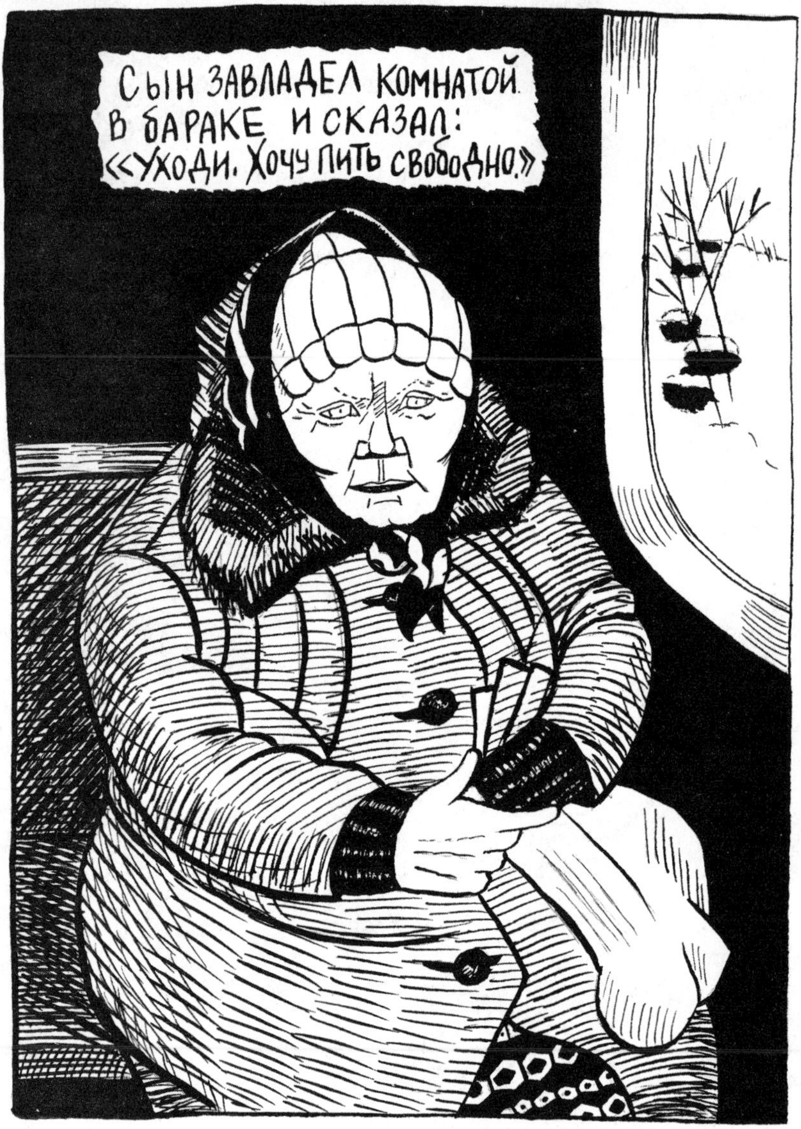
Сын завладел комнатой в бараке и сказал: «Уходи. Хочу пить свободно.»

"My son seized my room in the barracks and said, 'Go away. I want to drink freely.'"

This is how a former village schoolteacher began her story. Homeless, she travels from one old acquaintance to another, staying with them as long as they can stand her. She is also not welcome at the hospital. The doctors skimp on free medications, telling her she should "live less."

With no one else to listen to her, the old woman told her story to occasional fellow passengers. "A chickadee landed on my window today. That means I'll die soon."

"I'll be gone by the fall. A new dress, bloomers, and even a handkerchief are ready on the back of my chair."

A PRAYER AGAINST THE GENERAL PLAN

Every Saturday, rain, snow, or frost, a group of Orthodox activists holds a prayer service and protest rally against Moscow Mayor Yuri Luzhkov's urban planning policies. They are opposed to the construction of tunnels and a Turkish shopping mall under Pushkin Square in downtown Moscow. The square is the burial place of the monks of the Strastnoy Monastery, demolished in the 1930s as part of the general plan for the reconstruction of Moscow.

"Rejoice, raiment for the wretched and naked! Rejoice, nourishment for the poor and desolate!"

"The demons are horrified by our appearance here."

"Rejoice, unshakable pillar of the Church!"

"You had better pray pensions aren't cut."

"You had better pray against our presidents!"

"Pray against kikes? It won't help."

"Our prayers will melt the snow."

"Brothers and sisters, let us pray against the General Plan."

FEMININE

In "Feminine," all the characters are drawn from life, and their remarks are recorded verbatim.

However, I have tried to move away from reportage and toward symbolism in this series—to generalize specific situations in images that express my feelings and experiences.

The portraits here are not so much images of specific people as they are archetypes: the faded, lonely woman, the slutty boozer, the rigid old Soviet woman, and so on.

Each drawing adds its own tint (of sadness, irony, and anger) to the overall picture—the life of women in the Russian provinces.

"When I was young, I had a date lined up on every corner."

"There are no factories in this town, and no men."

"He couldn't just put on slippers and become domesticated."

"I've been feeling slutty since December."

I was born in Serpukhov, a town in the Moscow region. The women and girls I knew talked about men: acquaintances and strangers, exes, current husbands and boyfriends, future husbands and boyfriends. We believed that love would change the monotonous course of our lives.

I had one other belief—in my calling as an artist. Only my dad, a self-taught artist, supported my plan to study in Moscow and then work as an artist. Believing the nonsense I was spouting was infectious and a hindrance to finding a husband, some of my girlfriends' moms tried to force their daughters to spend less time with me. They were right: I'm still not married, and I don't have any children.

"I'm not sloshed. I'm a saint."

"We're used to the fellas paying for everything."

I have lived in Moscow for over a decade. When I travel to the provinces, the scenes I see and the conversations I hear are familiar to me. Even divorced girlfriends sympathize with my "bitter plight."

I became an artist, but I do not feel like a winner. In this country, these women's life strategies and mine are transformed into losses. I look at the heroines in "Feminine" and find a part of myself in all of them.

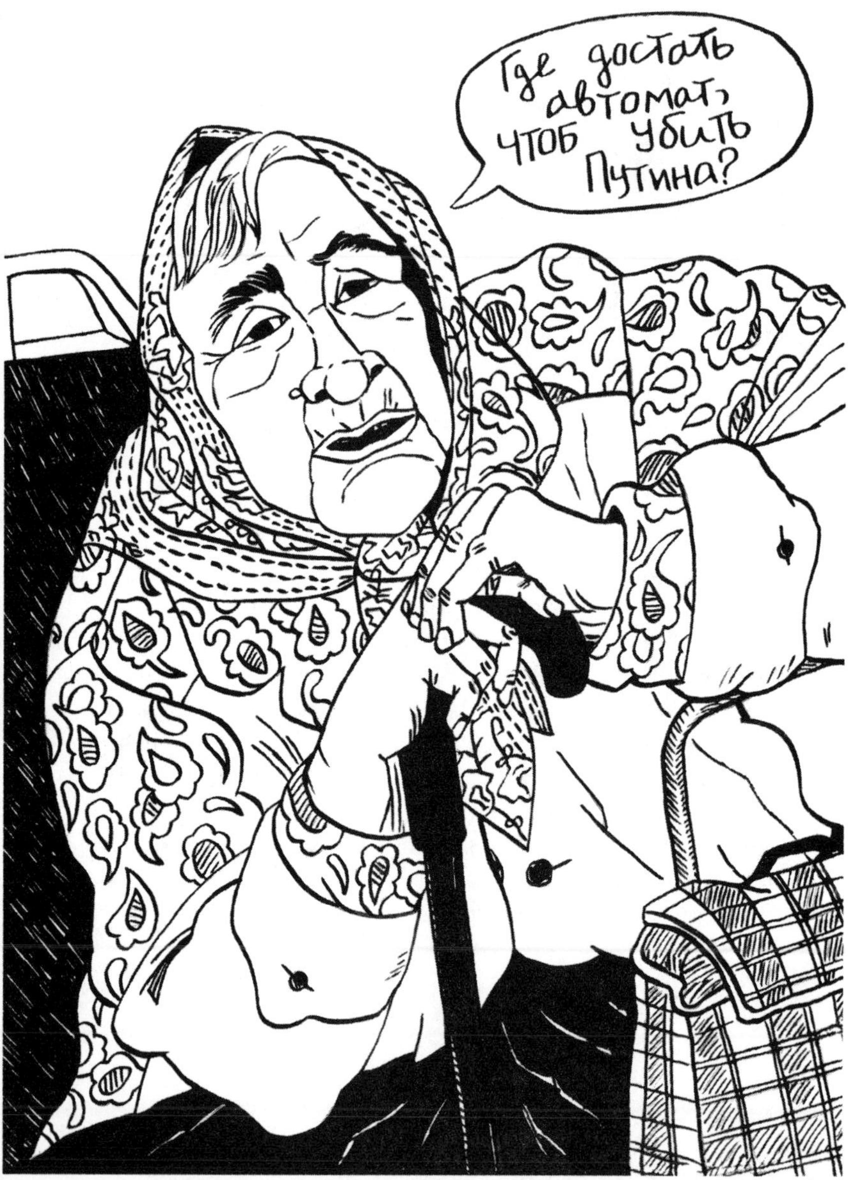
Где достать автомат, чтоб убить Путина?

"Where can I get hold of a machine gun to kill Putin?"

DRAWING LESSONS
AT A JUVENILE PRISON

In August 2010, I visited the Mozhaysk Juvenile Prison for the first time, as a volunteer for the Center for Prison Reform, and gave a drawing lesson to some of the inmates. I taught drawing classes at the girls' penitentiaries in Novy Oskol and Ryazan and the boys' penitentiary in Aleksin, but Mozhaysk is the only place I visited more or less regularly. I was originally trained as an educator, and before I came to Mozhaysk I prepared an experimental syllabus with ten lesson plans.

There was almost no funding for the trips. We traveled by commuter train, carrying everything we needed for classes in our backpacks, so, with rare exceptions, we used the simplest materials during the lessons: paper and black pens. The Center organized the trips once a month. If you missed a trip, you had to wait for the next time around.

There is a constant turnover of inmates at the juvenile prison. Some are released on parole, others are transferred to adult prisons, and new inmates show up all the time. Over a six-month period, the roster of my drawing groups changed completely.

Some of the teens were well educated, while others were hearing everything for the first time. Many of them had psychological problems. In short, teaching classes at a penitentiary was tricky: you had to experiment and develop your own lesson plans.

Why did we travel to the prisons? The Center's staff and volunteers bring clothing to inmates about to be released on parole, as well as hygiene products, birthday presents, and treats for the other inmates. Staff and volunteers also provide psychological assistance and gather information for publications aimed at troubled teens. The Center also recruits creative people willing to work regularly with the teens, who need interaction with people from the outside world no less than they need shampoo and socks.

I realize I cannot teach someone to draw when the lessons are so infrequent. My emphasis is on developing analytical thinking (structuring the drawing) and empathy (working on the image). It is also vital to help the kids gain self-confidence, so all of their work is shown at exhibitions. We photographed the exhibitions and brought the photos back to the prison to show the kids.

The kids found out about the drawing lessons from their minders, but more often they heard about them by word of mouth. Between five and ten students came to my classes. There is often a self-taught artist among them, someone who really wanted to learn to draw.

I continued the drawing lessons until 2014. I hoped that we could receive some kind of grant for the project, so that the trips would be more frequent, and so that we could publish a book with all the work we'd collected and developed over four years: the lesson plans, the student drawings, and the photographs of the exhibits. Unfortunately, funding became even harder to acquire, and access to the prison only became more constrained, so we were unable to publish the book. All the archival materials from the project are currently housed at the Museo Nacional Centro de Arte Reina Sofía in Madrid; I didn't want them to remain in Russia, where they could very well have disappeared, like so many materials from past social experiments.

"There are swastikas encoded in Raphael's drawings."

Oleg draws a lot. He has his own views of Renaissance masterpieces.

"Look over there—darkies!"
"Where?"
"Right there!"

Oleg is a skinhead. It all started when, at the age of 8, he witnessed the murder of a friend. Teenagers from the Caucasus killed him over his telephone. At 14, Oleg organized a "fight club," in which he was the youngest member. The fighters "staged flash mobs at Caucasian markets." In his small provincial town, Oleg said, the population was divided into skinheads, people from the Caucasus, and suckers. He was convicted of a gang killing. He expected to be rewarded for his patriotism, not punished. Oleg had kept up his spirits at the penitentiary by studying foreign languages, philosophy, and economics. He dreams of becoming a politician: "Yanukovych's priors didn't stop him from becoming president." In the fall, he was transferred to an adult prison.

ANDREI

"On the outside, lots of things keep a guy from wising up."

Andrei is a prison artist. He makes "bands"—pen-and-ink drawings on handkerchiefs and other pieces of cloth—a popular art form in Russian prisons. He wants to draw beautifully and with feeling, yet he despises formal exercises. But he did like the lecture on concentration camp drawings. He read Solzhenitsyn and taught himself to draw by copying illustrations in books from the local library. Andrei's sentence ended before the New Year, but no one was waiting for him on the outside when he was released.

"I'm drawing my anger at the world. Each drop is a grievance: it's like rain."

Yevgeny is a gambler. He was sent to the colony for busting open a slot machine. He didn't know how to draw and didn't want to learn: he came to class to get things off his chest. Yevgeny always looked tense. He hated his surroundings and once said he wanted to murder people. Oleg, the skinhead, took him down a peg. "Shut up. You don't know what murder is."

"On the outside, I drew cartoon characters."

Alexei is a tall and handsome teenager. He is well read and has a good memory. What he liked most during the lessons were the explanations of the abstract foundations of composition, which either irritated or dumbfounded the other inmates.

It was obvious the other boys avoided Alexei, and one of them half-jokingly called him a maniac. It turned out that once, on New Year's Eve, Alexei had committed a double murder while intoxicated. One of his victims had suffered approximately fifty stab wounds. Before the New Year, Alexei was transferred to an adult prison in Tambov, while the skinheads were sent to a prison in the Moscow region.

Human rights activist Natalia Dzyadko has worked with the penitentiary for eight years. Along with staff members at the Center for Prison Reform, she brings the inmates candy and presents on their birthdays, and she invites people willing to work with the boys to come to the prison. It is difficult to gain entry to the prison without outside help. There are exceptions, however. The famous actor and musician Pyotr Mamonov has been granted the right to visit any time, without a pass. He doesn't come that often, once or twice a year, but the inmates who have caught his concerts at the penitentiary still remember him.

"Why doesn't anyone come here and play soccer with the boys?"

The inmates have almost no time for themselves: their lives are organized around a strict schedule. But when they do have free time, what they like most of all is playing soccer.

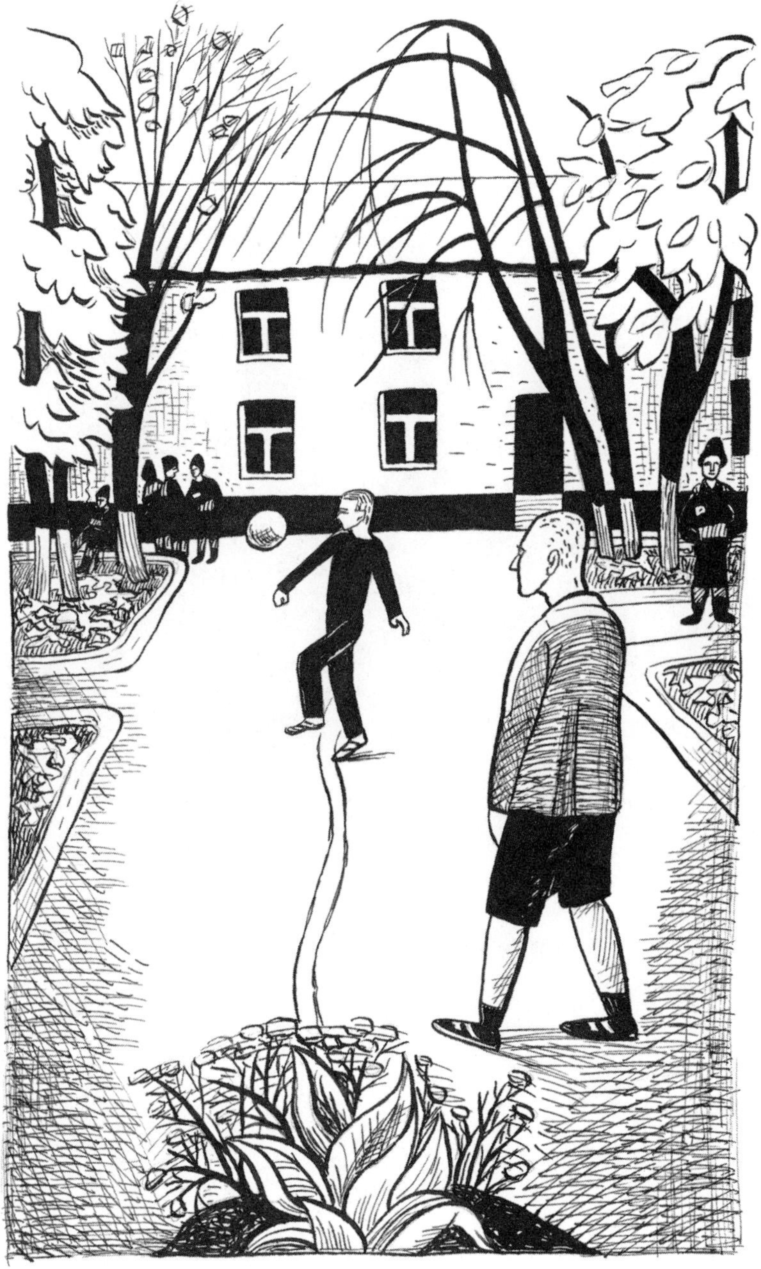

"We're fighting a plague! We're fighting the entire Russian narco-mafia."

Activists sometimes visit the penitentiary, including a band consisting of former alcoholics and drug addicts from the organization Transfiguring Russia. The musicians performed songs they had written about the benefits of a healthy lifestyle.

The boys said the concert was cool, but it was odd that the musicians were wearing slippers and torn socks.

"I'm going to sing you songs from the '80s."

Father Andrei, from The Descent of the Holy Spirit Church, also visited the inmates. The church is famous for its prior, the former rock musician Sergei Rybko. The priest performed several songs at a concert in the prison.

"God definitely needs all of us."

As in adult prisons, many inmates at the juvenile penitentiary turn to religion. There is a tiny wooden church on the premises. There are lots of icons in every residential unit, and even the TV in the common room is ringed with icons. Orthodox priests frequently come on the weekends to receive confession, chat, and show films about Russian Orthodoxy. No one comes to see the Muslim boys.

"They've put up a crooked New Year's tree for us, trimmed with crooked decorations."

As the New Year approached, there were few boys left at the penitentiary. Some had been released, while others had been transferred to adult prisons.

A VILLAGE SCHOOL

This is the school in the tiny village of Nikolskoye. You can get to the village by bus from Tula; the trip takes an hour and a half. There is no public transportation between Nikolskoye and the nearest large village, Krapivna, or the district center, Shchyokino. The locals rarely leave the village.

ZOYA NIKOLAYEVNA: "In four years, we've turned it into a normal school."
SERGEI ALEXANDROVICH: "The parents now see their children as human beings."

This is the school's director, Zoya Nikolayevna, and her husband, Sergei Alexandrovich, a teacher and the school's supply and maintenance manager. They live in Krapivna, and until 2008 they worked at the Krapivna boarding school for orphans and sick children. When the boarding school closed, Zoya Nikolayevna, Sergei Alexandrovich, and a team of Krapivna teachers transferred to the Nikolskoye school. Around eight in the morning, the couple leaves for work by car. Their drive takes them through hills, woods, and fields.

The road from Krapivna to Nikolskoye crosses the Upa River. In the spring, the Upa floods, completely submerging the bridge. During the floods, the Ministry of Emergency Situations arranges passage across the river. In the past, people were ferried on a military amphibious vehicle, which resembles a tank with no gun turret. Now they are ferried in a small motorboat. The motor constantly stalls, and the guy from the MES has to row all day from shore to shore, battling the strong current.

"It's been flooded for a month."

"There's no spare motor, dock, or field kitchen," the MES guy complained as he plied the oars, "but the top brass comes in an expensive helicopter and films everything on an expensive screen."

The teachers from Krapivna make the crossing twice a day.

"The children do calculations on their telephones. They have no use for mathematics."

There are twenty-three pupils and ten teachers at the Nikolskoye school. There are four pupils in the biggest grade, and one in the smallest. Several pupils commute from neighboring villages, where there are no schools. In summer, they ride their bicycles; in winter, they come on foot. When the roads are drifted over with snow, and the local authorities have not had time to clear them, they stay home.

The school in the neighboring village of Kuzmino remained open for a long time with a total of five pupils. There were more teachers than pupils. If there is no school, a village is doomed, the teachers say.

By way of comparison, there are no fewer than twenty pupils in each grade at the Krapivna village school, and a total of 226 in all.

In some classes, half the pupils are children of migrant workers. Families from Dagestan have been moving to Krapivna in large numbers and buying homes, while migrant workers from Central Asia settle in hostels on the outskirts of the town. They work in gardens and warehouses.

In the class pictured above, there were two Uzbek pupils, a Tajik, a Lezgin, and an Azerbaijani.

The children get along with each other.

"They're all local kids to me. We have a friendship of peoples here," said the teacher, smiling.

But there are problems, too. Some of the migrant children cannot speak Russian passably, and not all the children are sent to school at the right age: the Tajik boy I met was three heads taller than the other pupils. It turned out he had been enrolled in first grade at the age of 10.

For the time being, there are only ethnic Russian children at the Nikolskoye school—no migrants.

The village has a single employer, Nikolai Kurkov, former chairman of the Lenin Komsomol State Farm and now the owner of two farms, a grove, and a dairy. The parents of the pupils at the Nikolskoye school either work for Kurkov or have moved to Shchyokino or Tula, leaving their kids with their grandmothers.

The kindergarten in Nikolskoye closed back in the 1990s and, unless their grandmothers are there to raise them, the children turn into rural Mowglis.

There are two pupils in the first grade, but the teacher has a hard time coping with them.

"At the beginning of the school year, they ran around the classroom during lessons and screamed," she recounts.

It would be financially unfeasible to open a private kindergarten in the village. Nikolskoye residents wouldn't be able to pay the tuition fee—more than 1,000 rubles a month (approximately $26 at the time of writing) per child—to send their kids there.

TEACHER: "Is 'Moscow' a person's name or a place name?"
SASHA, A FIRST-GRADER: "It's a street."

The village school doesn't have a gym or a cafeteria. A kitchen has been set up behind the bookshelf in the most spacious classroom. The tables there are set when the children have lunch. They are fed buckwheat kasha, macaroni, and rice with gravy; sausages or beef cutlets; and a delicious compote. The grandmother of one of the pupils, a former employee of Kurkov's dairy, works as the cook.

A chauffeur drives the village's gilded youth, Kurkov's numerous grandchildren, to a better-equipped school in Shchyokino.

On May 9, Victory Day, the pupils at the Nikolskoye school put on a holiday concert under the direction of the music and physical education teacher. Guests arrived: two war veterans, who had gotten tipsy for the occasion; two female graduates of the school; three old women; and an elderly former teacher who cried throughout the concert.

"These are the victims who have come to life from the ashes and risen once again, and risen once again!"

The older pupils have been touched by World War II. Many of their grandparents have told them how the fascists marched through Nikolskoye when they were children. But the kids see other events in Russian history as dry, boring facts in textbooks.

The first-graders do not know our country's capital.

"Well, and so what?" winces their teacher, who considers Moscow a big dump.

Indeed, so what? The residents of the capital are also largely uninterested in the life and death of lost villages like Nikolskoye.

SLAVES OF MOSCOW

On October 30, 2012, a group of civil society activists in Moscow freed twelve slaves from Produkty, a grocery store owned by a Kazakhstani couple, Zhansulu Istanbekova and her husband, Saken Muzdybayev. Nearly all of the freed slaves were women from the city of Shymkent, Kazakhstan, which is Istanbekova's hometown. Istanbekova had invited them to Moscow to work in her store. Once there, they had been robbed of their passports and forced to work without pay for twenty hours a day. They were fed slop made from rotten vegetables, and they were beaten and raped. Some of the freed women had arrived at the store recently, but others had been slaves there for as long as ten years.

Many of them had given birth while in captivity. Istanbekova had disposed of the children as she saw fit. She shipped some of them to Kazakhstan, later declaring them dead, while others had served her family from an early age.

Tazhinar Ashirova had been trying to free her daughter, Zarina, for several years. She had failed to get the police in Kazakhstan to open a criminal case. The Golyanovo police precinct in Moscow had also ignored Tazhinar's written complaint.

According to the former slaves, the police had known what was happening at the store and had regularly come to Istanbekova to ask for bribes. When slaves would run away, the police would bring them back to their proprietress. Realizing she could not rescue her daughter through legal channels, Tazhinar had turned to activists from the Alternativa movement, who succeeded in freeing the slaves during a surprise mass raid on the store.

Zhansulu's two sisters were also believed to have been involved in slavery. Each of them also owns several stores, places where slavery has probably flourished for the past twenty-five years or so. Zhansulu's older sister, Sholpan, was convicted of torture in 2002. However, guided by "humane" considerations, President Vladimir Putin granted her a pardon in 2003.

In November 2012, Istanbekova and Muzdybayev were charged with false imprisonment, but the case against them was later dismissed as "illegal and groundless." The couple reopened the Produkty grocery store immediately after the New Year, and they are currently recruiting people to work there.

The topic of modern slavery has long interested me. After reading an article on the internet about the freeing of the Produkty slaves, I called the Civic Assistance Committee to offer my services as an artist during the trial against slaveholders Istanbekova and Muzdybayev. Anastasia Denisova, a Committee staffer, told me the latest news. The women were supposed to have had a face-to-face confrontation with their former bosses at the Preobrazhenskoe police investigative department. Instead, police had tried to cook up a misdemeanor charge against the victims (for residing in the country illegally, without registering their place of residence) in order to quickly deport them back to Kazakhstan and Uzbekistan.

BAKIYA: "An acquaintance told me the conditions and pay would be good."

One of the young women, five months pregnant, nearly had a miscarriage. Activists and the victims' lawyers had managed to get them out of the investigative department and take them to a hospital.

After hearing this story, I went to the hospital, where I met Leila and Mutabar.

Leila, from Uzbekistan, is 26 years old. She has spent ten of those years in bondage.

ПРЕ СТУПНИКИ
НА ВОЛЕ,
ПОЛИЦИЯ НЕ СОБИРАЕТСЯ
ИХ ЛОВИТЬ,
ЗАТО КАЖДЫЙ ДЕНЬ
ДОПРАШИВАЮТ НАС.

"The criminals are at large, and the police have no intention of arresting them. But they interrogate us every day."

A volunteer guarded the young women. The former slaves were taken from the hospital to the Civic Assistance Committee's office. The wind outside was so strong it even blew through my leather coat, while the pregnant Leila slipped over the frosty pavement in flats and a windbreaker. She had no hat or gloves. She clung to me to avoid falling—and for warmth.

The hungry young women ate fast food at Metro Express. Then they cuddled up to each other and instantly fell asleep.

BAKIYA

Bakiya is 34, but she could pass for 40. She has spent ten years in slavery, enduring daily beatings to the head and kidneys. Her front teeth have been knocked out, her fingers are broken, and her ears torn.

Bakiya's son, Baurzhan, is 5 years old, but he looks as if he were 2. The boy has a hard time walking: his rib cage is deformed. Until his release, Baurzhan had never been outdoors. Doctors believe he may have been set on a pot and tied to a radiator all day long. Baurzhan talks a lot, but no one knows the language: maybe he invented it. His mother saw him once every six months for half an hour. Bakiya also gave birth to a daughter in captivity, a girl who would now be around 7 years old. Zhansulu Istanbekova told her the girl had died, but Bakiya thinks she is alive, that she was sold and sent to Kazakhstan.

Bakiya said there were at least thirty security cameras in the Produkty store, and the slaves were not allowed to stray outside their range. They were forbidden to talk to each other. The workday began at six in the morning and lasted until late at night.

They were often beaten unconscious, and sometimes the beatings would continue even after they had passed out.

"I won't settle down until I see blood," Istanbekova would say.

The owners' four sons were often present during the beatings. These teenagers had themselves begun pummeling their "property," which their parents encouraged.

"We had two minutes to eat. When we didn't finish in time, they'd beat us on the head with billy clubs."

BAKIYA WITH HER MOTHER, TUMAR: "The boss lady said, 'Even if they put me behind bars, my people will kill some of you.'"

The owners made the slaves inform on each other. Bakiya says that she refused to be a stool pigeon and kept her mouth shut during beatings, trying to resist. The store also had a system whereby the slaves had to "matchmake" one of their relatives—that is, lure them into bondage—in order to live more or less tolerably. Bakiya had not invited anyone to "earn good money."

Bakiya once managed to escape. She slept in a stairwell for three days before going outside, where she ran into a regular customer from Produkty. Bakiya told the woman her story and begged for help. The customer took Bakiya home and told her to wait. After a while, the customer came back with Istanbekova. Istanbekova swore that Bakiya's slave labor would be compensated, that they would even buy her a car. I don't know whether Bakiya believed this or not, but she remembered her hostage son and returned to the store. Of course, back at the store, she was beaten for running away, and everything continued as usual.

The activists working the case discovered that the Istanbekov sisters enjoy a fairly high social standing, and have connections among government officials and police.

В МИЛИЦИИ
В УЗБЕКИСТАНЕ
МНЕ СКАЗАЛИ:
« УЗНАВАЙТЕ АДРЕС,
ОСВОБОЖДАЙТЕ
САМИ77,

TUMAR, TO A LAWYER: "The police in Uzbekistan told me, 'Find the address and free her yourself.'"

Bakiya is from a large, poor Kazakh family in Uzbekistan. Several years ago, one of Istanbekova's escaped slaves got in touch with Tumar and told her that her daughter was in bondage. Tumar called the police, but they refused to conduct an investigation, and she failed to raise the money for a ticket to Moscow.

LEILA'S FAMILY

Bakhyt, Leila's son, was born in captivity. His name means "happiness." He is 6 years old.

Istanbekova took his sister, also born in captivity, to Kazakhstan, and some time later told Leila the girl had been killed. She said a cow had gored her to death.

Bakhyt was left to live in the store. He became something like a plaything for one of the owners' sons, who was his age. When he was not entertaining the son, Bakhyt had to work: he packed and carried groceries and gave the boss massages. When the boy made mistakes, Istanbekova or her assistant Beka would beat his head against the wall or against an iron safe. The boy has scars on his head from his beatings at the hands of his owners. Bakhyt saw Leila every day, but was forbidden from communicating with her.

When the slaves were released, Istanbekova abducted Bakhyt and the other children, but fearing press attention, she abandoned them at a train station. Bakhyt wants to watch cartoons all day. Leila says the boy now smiles and even goofs off from time to time.

In 2011, a husband, Seilkhan, came into Leila's life. He had arrived from Kazakhstan and was working for a relative of Istanbekova's when he happened to meet Leila. Noticing Leila really liked Seilkhan, Istanbekova invited him to become the store's driver and settle in the basement with Leila and the other slaves. Seilkhan took the offer. Unlike the other workers, however, he was paid a salary and not beaten, because, as a driver, he could escape.

SEILKHAN AND LEILA: "Istanbekova decided that we should bear slaves for her."

Leila is now seven months pregnant. An ultrasound has shown that, despite the constant beatings she suffered, the child is all right. Leila believes that Istanbekova planned for her and her husband to work at Produkty into their old age (or until their deaths), and for their children to become her slaves. Leila did not think about escaping, because she feared for Bakhyt and did not want to abandon him.

LEILA: "Zhansulu believes that money decides everything."

Zhansulu Istanbekova was from a poor family, says Leila. The other freed women say that Istanbekova launched her criminal career managing brothels in Kazakhstan. Only a distant relative of her husband, whom Istanbekova had held in bondage for seventeen years, knew everything about Zhansulu's past. The relative, named Saltanat, had abandoned two children born into slavery and had fled right before the liberation of the Golyanovo slaves. The freed women say she had promised to save the others and contact them.

But this had not happened. The former slaves surmise that Saltanat had been captured and killed because she was much too dangerous as a witness. Besides, there had been little use for her at the store. Leila and Seilkhan described her condition. Her hair had fallen out; her legs were purple from constant beatings ("At first we thought she was wearing purple tights"); and blood often spurted from big lumps on her legs.

Saltanat's daughter, Asel, never got an education. She'd worked as a servant for Istanbekova's mother since she was a small child, which meant that she was a second-generation slave. She could not imagine what freedom and life without an owner were like.

ZARINA AND TAZHINAR

Zarina is Leila's niece. Leila was the first to be enslaved by the Istanbekovs. Four years later, Zhansulu forced her to invite a relative to Moscow through coercion, beatings, physical violence, and, most important, the threat of separating her from Bakhyt, who was then a newborn. The 14-year-old Zarina was told she would work at Produkty during school holidays, but the girl wound up a slave for six years.

TAZHINAR, ZARINA, AND ZARINA'S SON

Zarina was born in Uzbekistan to a Kazakh family. After her husband's death, Zarina's mother moved with her four children to Shymkent as part of a repatriation program for ethnic Kazakhs. Life wasn't easy for Tazhinar; a single mother, she had to rent an apartment and work at a construction site. There was never any money, and Zarina, who was the oldest, wanted to help her mother. Aside from paying the rent, she had to keep her younger sisters fed.

Tazhinar found out about the situation at the store. In Kazakhstan, she hired a lawyer. It turned out he had heard about Zhansulu Istanbekova: several escaped slaves had tried, unsuccessfully, to have charges filed against her. Tazhinar's attempt to file charges failed as well. She, her lawyer, and the other plaintiffs in the case are convinced that Balabiyev Kairat, a former prosecutor and now head of customs in Kazakhstan, helped quash the criminal case. According to them, Kairat was Istanbekova's lover and her patron.

ZARINA, TO A CIVIC ASSISTANCE COMMITTEE LAWYER:
"Balabiyev Kairat's people took me to a police station and forced me to sign a complaint against Mom."

When Istanbekova realized that Tazhinar would stop at nothing to rescue her daughter from captivity, she decided to intermarry their families. She forced Zarina to marry her own nephew, who abandoned a wife and two children in Kazakhstan. Nursultan was born from this marriage. Fearing the campaign that had arisen in defense of the Produkty slaves, the child's father had gone on the lam.

—

Like the other young women, Zarina refused to talk about other instances of violence in the presence of witnesses. They would only talk with the lawyers one-on-one.

"The boss lady ordered the guard, Beka, to break the fingers on both my hands."

"The police knew what was happening at the store."

The women said that police regularly visited the store. A policeman named Nasif was given 10,000 rubles at a time, while a policeman named Dima received 15,000 rubles (at the time, approximately $300 and $450, respectively).

MUTABAR

Mutabar is Muslim and sometimes wears a locket with a tiny Koran inside it. In Uzbekistan, she graduated from drama school, as well as a religious institution where she learned Arabic.

Mutabar is afraid that the police will abduct her and give her back to her "owners." At the Civic Assistance Committee, Mutabar identifies Istanbekova's relatives involved in the slavery case.

Mutabar wrote this inscription on my drawing:

Why don't the police help us? Where do people turn when they have been deceived as we have? Does money really decide everything nowadays?

Mutabar's story differs from those of the other liberated slaves.

Mutabar is an aspiring pop singer from Uzbekistan. Zhansulu Istanbekova personally invited her to come to Moscow to "be in a video," and Mutabar, overjoyed, took her up on her offer. She arrived in Moscow unable to speak Russian and not knowing her way around the city.

When she got to Produkty, she was told there would be no video shoot, and all her belongings were confiscated, including her passport, her telephone, and her laptop.

Istanbekova let it slip to the other slaves she was planning to sell Mutabar as a sex slave to some Arabs for good money. Only the intervention of the activists who liberated the women had prevented the deal from going through.

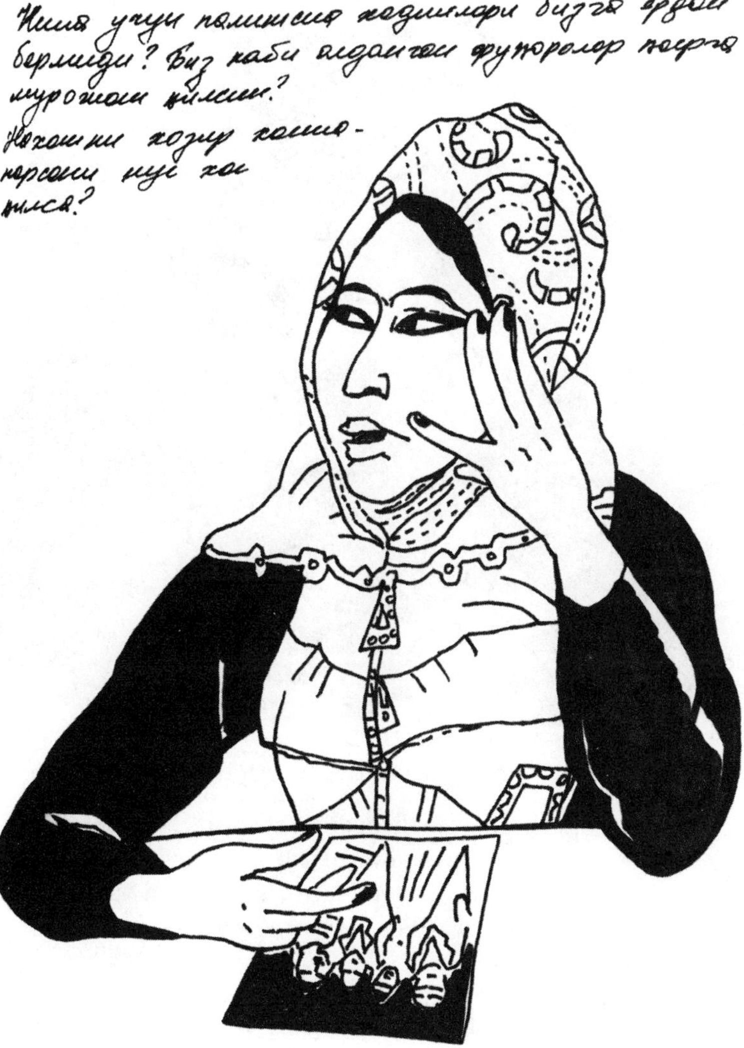
Нима учун полиция ходимлари бизга ёрдам бермиди? Биз каби алданган фуқаролар кимга мурожат қилсин?
Нахотки хозир хоким-ларсиз иш хал қилса?

I saw photographs taken in the apartment of Istanbekova's mother. The apartment had been renovated, but wasn't incredibly luxurious. The Istanbekovs have several such apartments in Moscow and in Shymkent, where Zhansulu also owns a mansion in the city's swanky neighborhood.

The elder Istanbekova is 101 years old. Some of the children born in slavery were sent to her to work as servants.

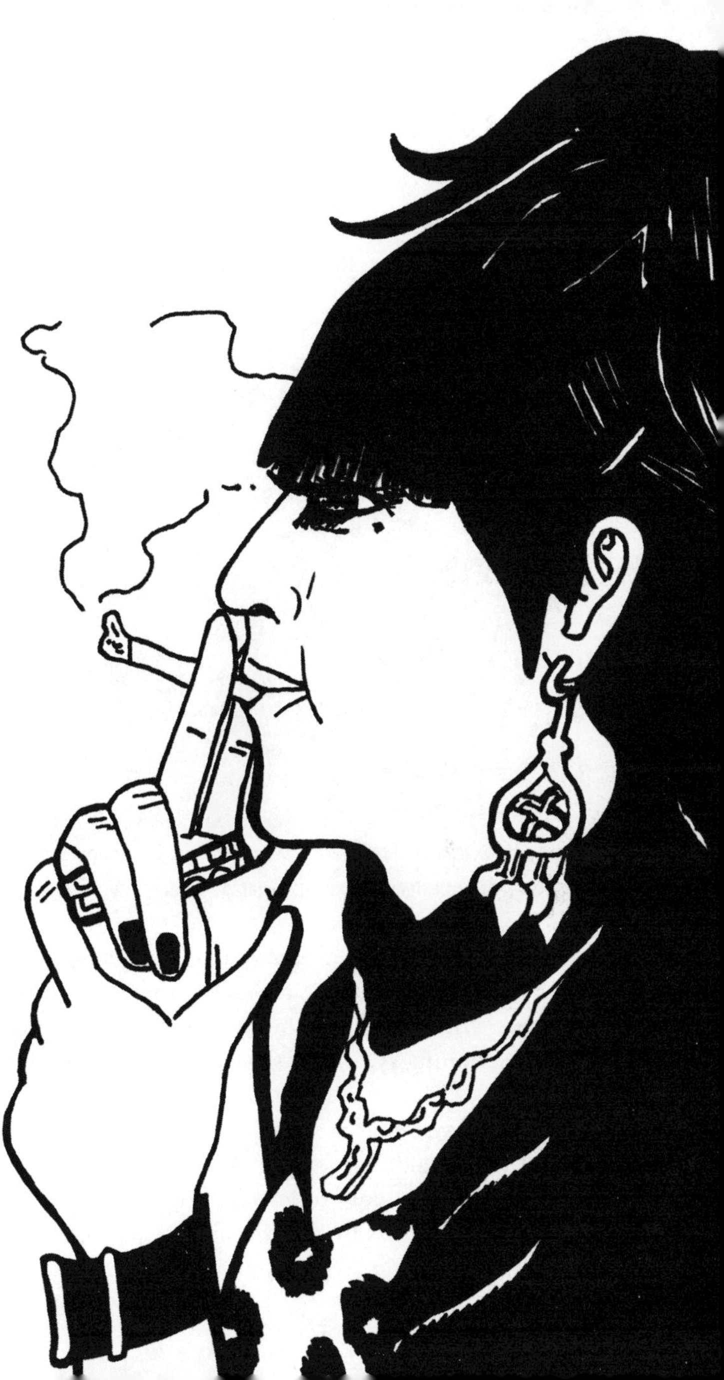

On December 11, 2012, a press conference entitled "The Case of the Freed Slaves: Developments in the Case and New Victims of the Slave Owners" was held at the Independent Press Center in Moscow.

SVETLANA GANNUSHKINA: "We hold press conferences where we report that nothing is happening. That is the main message."

During the press conference, Svetlana Gannushkina, head of the Civic Assistance Committee, repeatedly underscored the fact that the slaves owned by the Istanbekov clan were an ordinary case in a well-functioning system of slave trading and slave ownership in Russia.

"An entire system is at work. An investigation of it could lead us very far," she said.

At the moment, only activists, Civic Assistance Committee staffers, and journalists are involved in this dangerous investigation.

"A threat was passed along to Committee staffers via the prosecutor's office," Gannushkina told the assembled journalists. "We were told not to get mixed up in this case."

An interesting part of the press conference was a conversation, via Skype, with Zhanar Istanbekova's former slaves. Zhanar is the middle sister, and she is every bit the equal of Sholpan and Zhansulu. The escaped slaves had filed written complaints against Zhanar, but soon became convinced that the Istanbekov clan was omnipotent in their native Shymkent, and that it was useless to fight them. The women are now getting help from the Kazakhstani human rights organization Sana Sezim.

Istanbekova has been putting a lot of pressure on the victims and their relatives, alternately threatening them and offering them money, apartments, cars, yachts, etc. But she has also given an interview to Kazakhstani TV Channel 31, in which she said that Leila, Bakiya, and the other former shop clerks were extorting money from her.

After the press conference, I chatted with Leila and Bakiya. I asked them whether they were getting out and about in Moscow.

"Yes, we get out," Leila replied. "We go to hospitals every day."

LEILA, BAKIYA, AND ANASTASIA DENISOVA

BEFORE THE HOLIDAYS

In order to initiate criminal proceedings against the slave owners, some of the victims had to stay in Moscow. Leila and her family were settled in a rented apartment. Bakiya and Baurzhan were put up in a hostel.

On the eve of the New Year's holidays, some friends and I decided to take Bakiya and Baurzhan to a pizzeria, because they almost never go outdoors and rarely communicate with people. In her two months of freedom, Bakiya hasn't managed to go anywhere but Red Square—and to explore the route from her hiding place to the hospital, where Baurzhan has been undergoing tests. Because Istanbekova is at liberty, it is dangerous to go out.

Baurzhan would only have tea. He still refuses all food except dairy products. After peering into all the teapots on the table and touching the tea in his own cup with his hands, the boy continued to explore the new space. Now that he is not tied to a radiator all day, it is impossible to make him sit still. Baurzhan was intrigued by the New Year's decorations, and one of the waitresses let him remove a red plastic bulb from the tree. The child immediately started kicking the ball between the tables—his first time playing soccer.

Many diners cast puzzled glances at the little immigrant boy, who played oddly and awkwardly with his "ball." Baurzhan would laugh loudly and then, for no apparent reason, his facial expression would change and, frightened and on the verge of tears, he would run to his mother and cling to her. At some point, the bulb rolled down the stairs, and the child crawled down the steps. It is painful for him to walk down and, especially, up stairs the usual way. His leg was broken when he was in bondage, and the bones have not grown back together correctly.

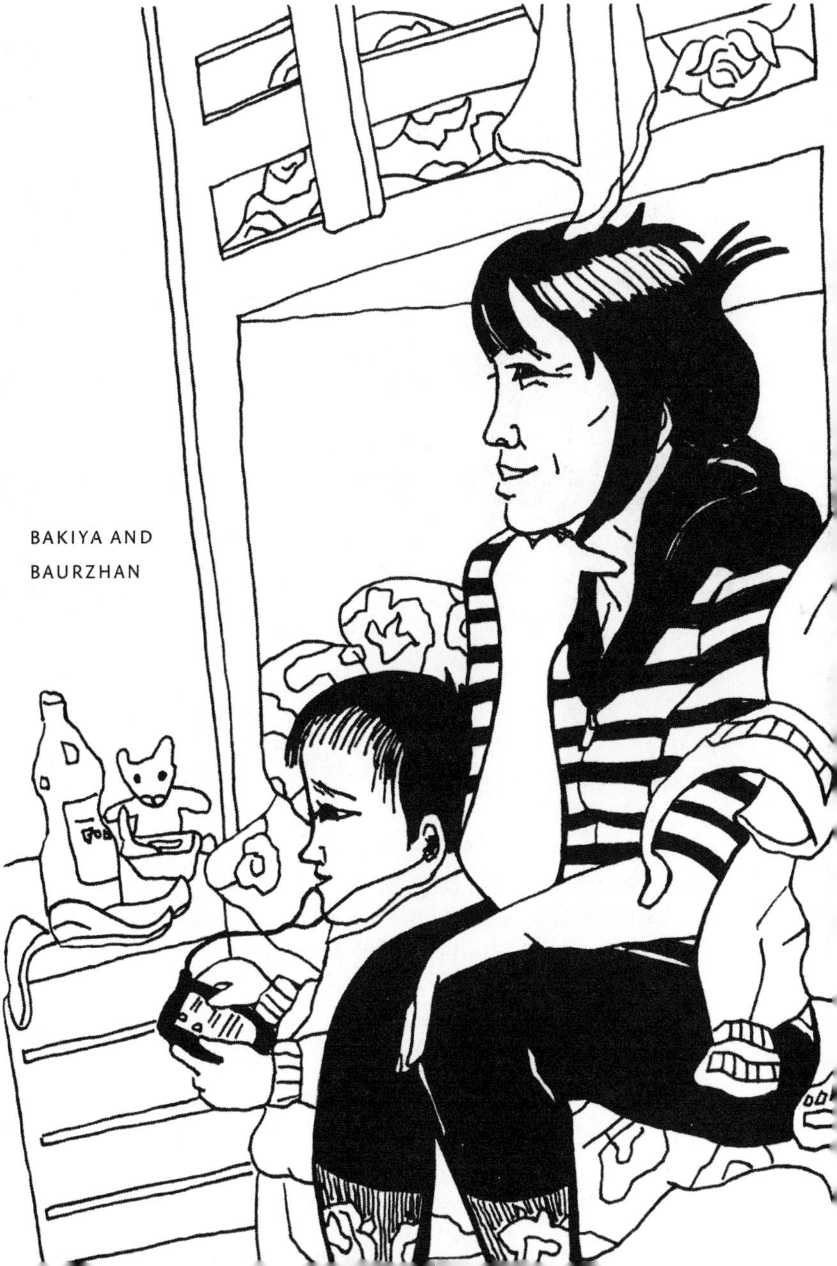

BAKIYA AND
BAURZHAN

Bakiya had obviously put on weight. She looked rejuvenated and bore little resemblance to the harried, wilted woman I remembered from early November. She joked and laughed a lot, unembarrassed by her toothless mouth.

Bakiya has dreams.

"I am going to work a lot. I am going to send Baurzhan off to my mother in Uzbekistan, and I will send them money. I also want to see the world, to go to Paris, to America. A person should see everything in life!"

We smiled shyly as we listened to Bakiya. Under the existing system, migrant workers are destined for slavery in one form or another, not for trips to Paris.

A few hours later, my friends and I had to run to other meetings. Bakiya did not want to leave. She wanted to go dancing or to go vist somewhere else. A jacket donated by activists was put on Baurzhan. A volunteer bodyguard who accompanied mother and child during the entire outing picked the boy up. We said goodbye.

THE GIRLS OF NIZHNY NOVGOROD

I got into contact with the "girls"—sex workers—with help from a social activist in Nizhny Novgorod named Andrei Amirov.

I was able to spend between five and fifteen minutes at each "office"—a rented apartment where sexual services are provided—during breaks between clients. I had to draw the series very quickly, on the spot, without making corrections. We made the rounds of over a dozen of these so-called offices.

It is nearly impossible for outsiders (especially women who are not working girls) to get into these offices. It was a valuable experience for me. I was able to make portraits, write down the women's own words, and ask them questions. There is a striking difference between the images of prostitutes circulated by the media and the working girls I saw. They condemned the violent behavior of men (not just their clients), harshly criticized the authorities (both government officials and the police), and tried to maintain personal boundaries even while doing this kind of work, which seemed wildly unrealistic to me.

I recalled times when men had subjected me to emotional and physical violence, but I had gone on claiming that this was what "normal" life was like.

When they are not busy, the working girls, the madam, and the so-called dispatcher hang out in the kitchen, behind a closed door or a curtain, while customers are served in the "chambers."

While I was making my way to the kitchen in different offices, I'd catch a glimpse of these rooms. The rooms all look alike: a sagging foldout couch or ottoman, a rug on the floor, a TV in the corner. Although the women keep the rooms clean, they are still alienating spaces: you can tell no one lives there. The chambers had been spruced up in only one of the offices I visited. The walls were hung with long, pale green curtains that, apparently, were meant to remind one of a boudoir.

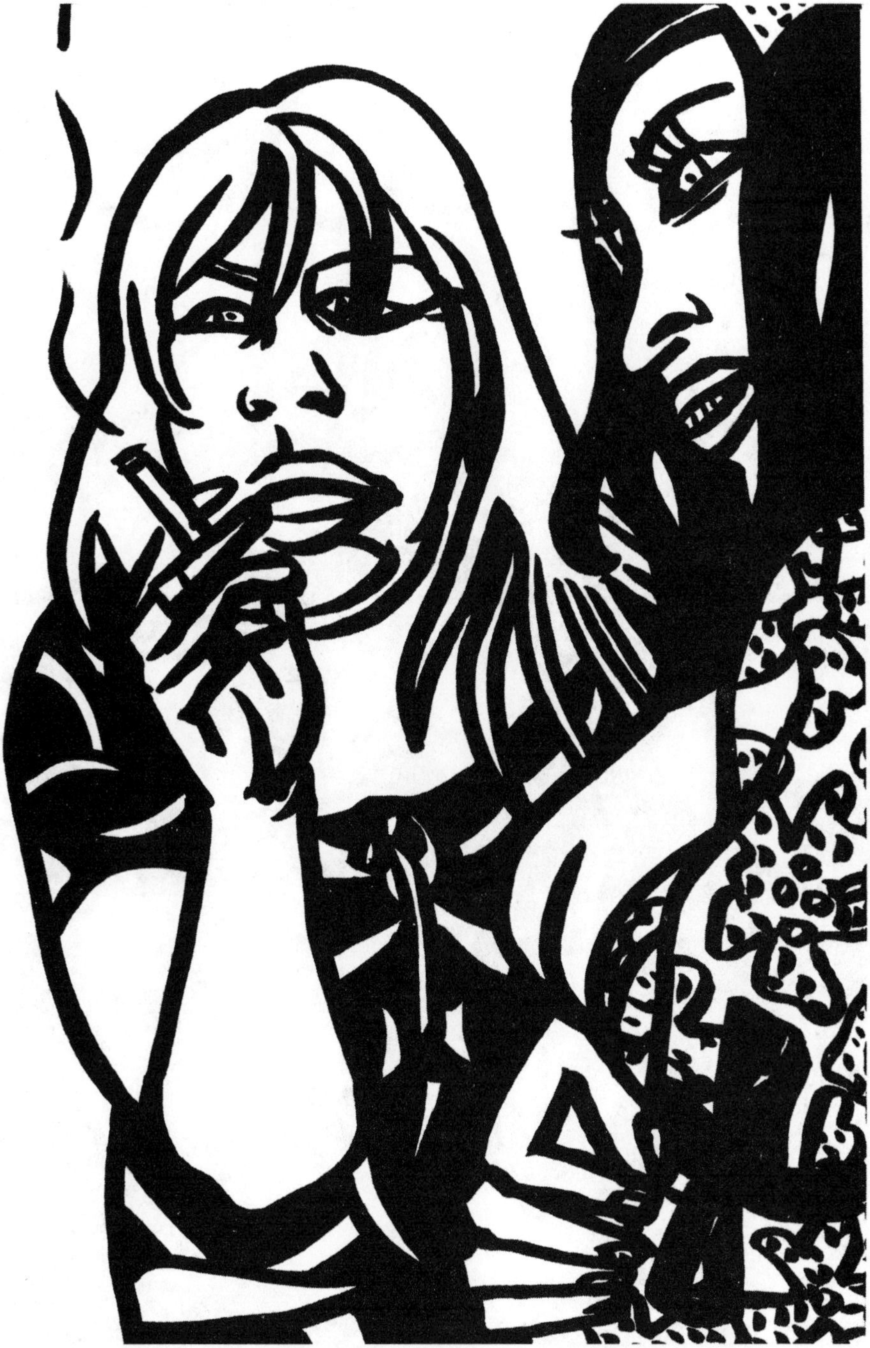

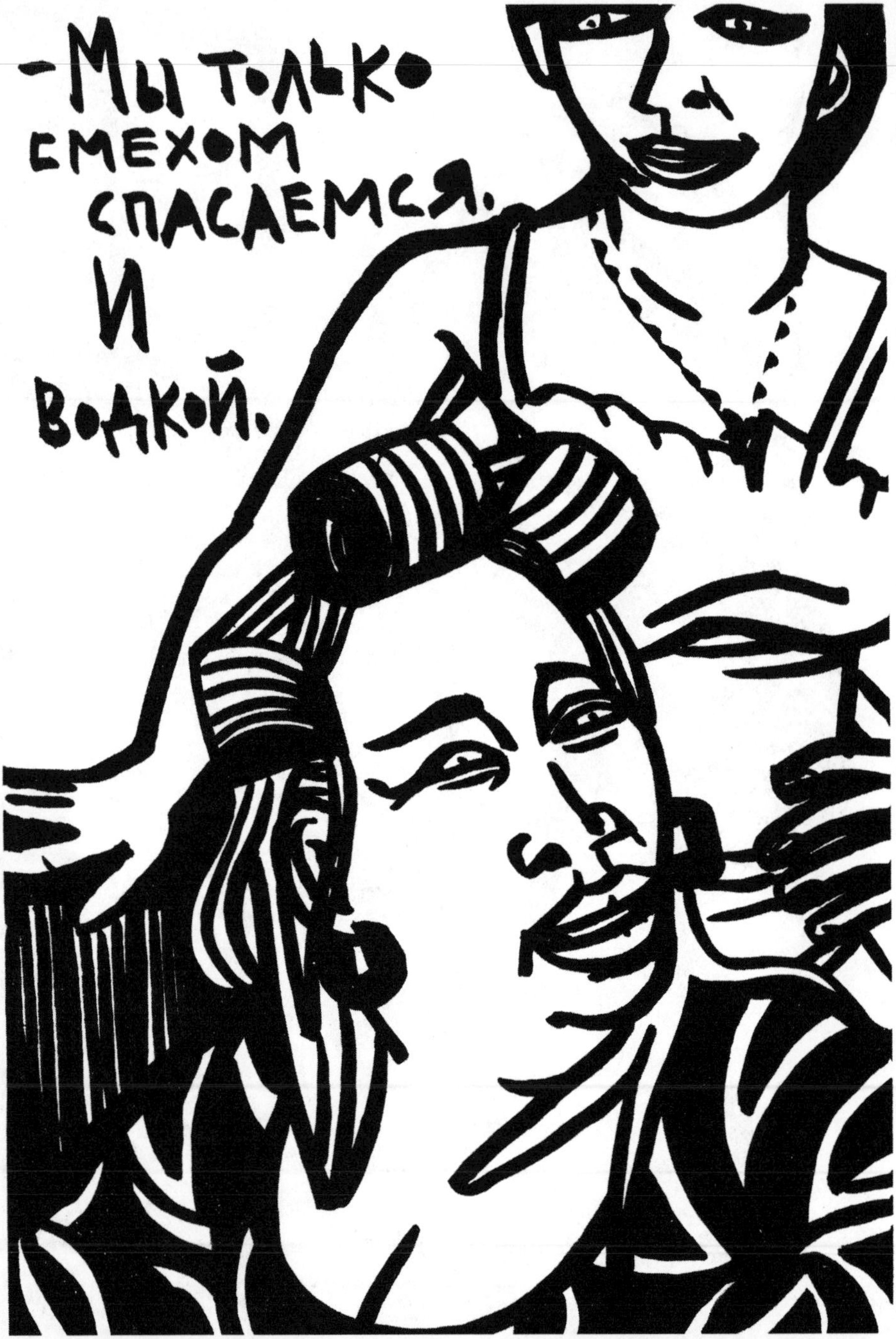
– Мы только смехом спасаемся. И водкой.

"Laughter is our only salvation. And vodka."

The women can quit working at a particular office at any moment. There were no pimps in the places I visited, though as an artist, of course, I would not have found myself in criminal haunts where women are held forcibly. As I understood from my brief interaction with the girls, such places are mainly located in Moscow.

The women frequently switch offices, and they come and go according to their own schedule. In a month, they earn between 30,000 and 60,000 rubles (at the time, between approximately $900 and $1,800). Many are married and work part time with their husbands' consent. Most of them have children. Some hold down legitimate jobs at the same time. Many of them support their husbands or boyfriends.

"When you set the table," one woman advised another, "tell him, 'Bon appetit! I nearly choked on a cock to pay for that.'"

One such lady, who was supporting her third or fourth husband, boasted that she would be going to the sea for the first time that summer.

The women who work in the offices all look different. There are young women with T-shirts, ponytails, and almost no makeup. There are the so-called "dames"—fortysomething and even fiftysomething—in corsets or velvet dresses with plunging necklines. Some women wear robes with nothing on underneath, a cigarette perpetually dangling from their lips. One not-so-young girl in a polka-dot cotton dress sat in the kitchen reading a dog-eared Soviet book. Most of the women looked slightly unkempt and tired, and wore modest, homey clothing.

One girl commented on the appearance of a workmate.

"Although she's 35, she looks like she's 50, but she keeps working at the office. You can't make her stay away or put on any clothes."

"It's a normal life. And an abnormal one, too."

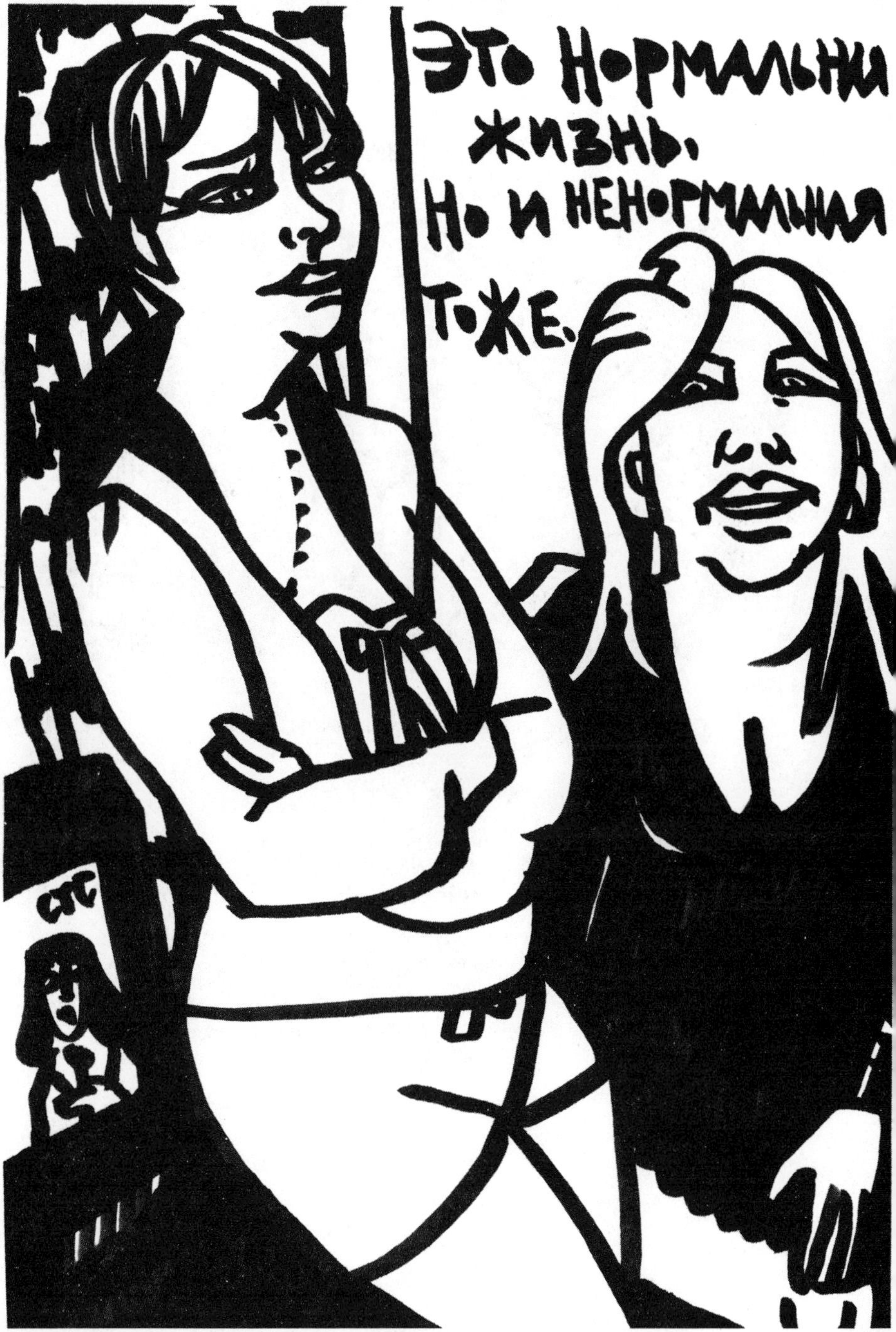
ЭТО НОРМАЛЬНИ
ЖИЗНЬ.
НО И НЕНОРМАЛЬНАЯ
ТОЖЕ.
СТС

"They're haggling again. They want a wholesale discount."

"This isn't a vegetable warehouse."

The madams act as team leaders, organizing the entire process. Madams are often former working girls themselves, and some of them continue to provide sexual services.

A new type of madam has emerged recently: energetic young women who have never worked as prostitutes, they simply run the offices and take a cut of the profits. There are also cases when the girls are self-organized and work without madams.

"The charge is 2,000 rubles an hour."

Each team also has a dispatcher, a woman who answers phone calls from customers. At some offices, the girls take turns working as dispatchers.

— Некоторые клиенты просят, чтобы на них ссали, а я бы с удовольствием срала. За всех женщин.

According to the girls, their clients are either "losers" or "darkies." When there are a lot of clients, they joke that there must be a holiday at the mental hospital.

"We know men backwards and forwards. Men are jerks."

"All of them?"

"No. There are players, too. They're like dogs: they want to get out of the house and live it up."

"Who are the strangest customers?"

"The ones who show up wearing women's lingerie, and who want to do a striptease themselves and get fucked with a strap-on. Many guys come here because their wives refuse to do fairly simple things. Customers sometimes offer to buy girls in bulk at a discount. Everyone wants a freebie."

"Some clients ask us to piss on them, but I'd be happy to shit on them, on behalf of all women."

The dames, the older women, are more loyal to their customers than the younger working girls are to theirs. Many dames have married former customers. Customers often visit the older women just to have a drink and a chat. They are charged separately for this.

Some working girls are willing to service people with disabilities. This is considered exceptional professionalism. The parents of a young man with cerebral palsy used to send holiday greetings to a woman who had agreed to provide their son with sexual services, regarding her as almost a member of the family.

> "Many guys come just to talk. We need to raise the fee for chats. Our brains are worth more."

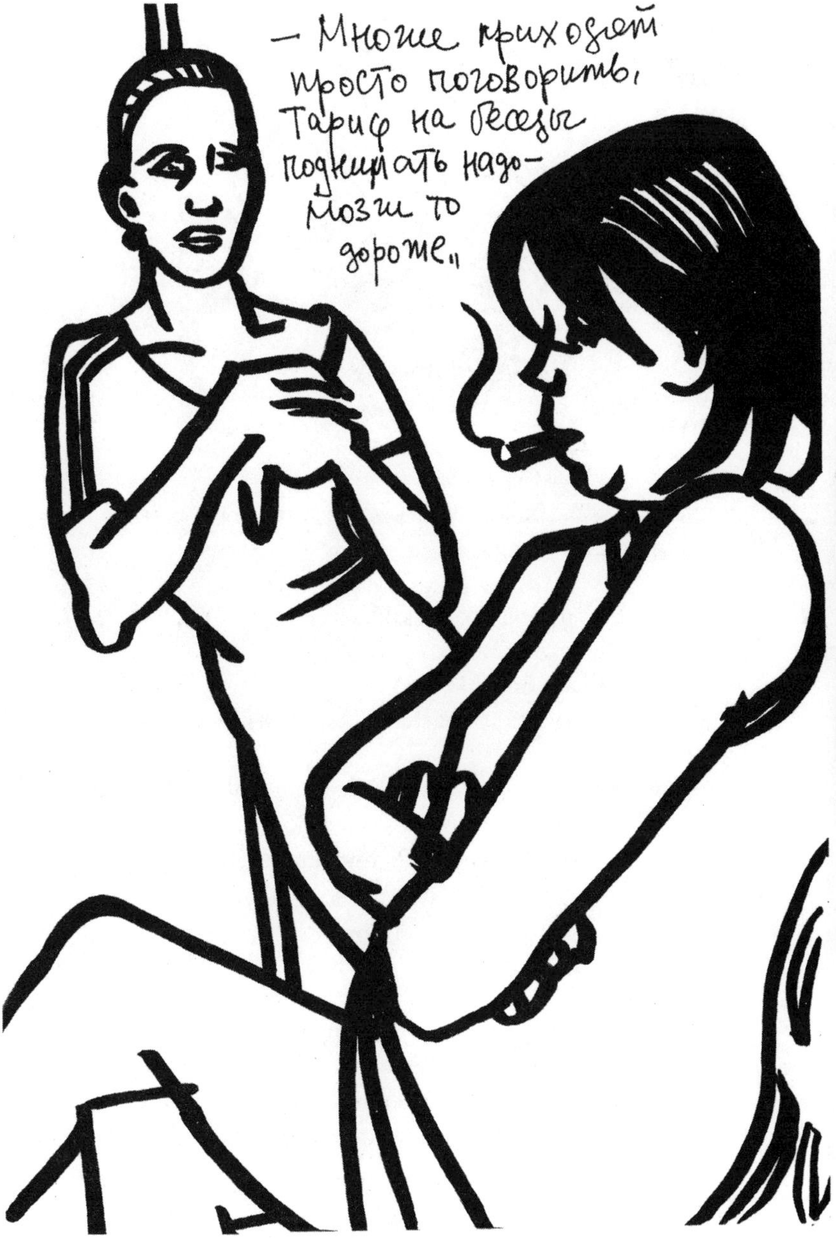
— Многие приходят просто поговорить, Тариф на беседы поднимать надо — мозги то дороже"

"Two of our dames married clients."

"Where else can you find a husband when you're past 45? You're not going to hit the clubs, are you?"

"Does life ever pan out for girls, like in *Pretty Woman*?"

The working girls laugh.

"Rich men are only like that in the movies! In real life, they're like that until the first quarrel. Then they remind us of all our faults."

Some girls end up as kept women, but they usually earn no more than they would working at an office. The men who pay the women can require them to do any number of things, including altering the way they look, completely isolating themselves from society, and bearing children for them. "She's now sitting at home like a dog," the girls said of a former comrade, whom a married client keeps isolated in a rented apartment, constantly forcing her to lose weight and change her appearance to look like a boy. I remarked that this sort of control of women and coercion also existed in ordinary families. All the women agreed with me. It was clear that many of them had experienced this firsthand.

"It's just a service."

Do the working girls want their profession legalized? I asked this question in every office I visited, and got very different answers. The girls who had been to Europe liked the way prostitution is treated in some countries there, as a normal paid service.

One girl told me she had worked in Germany, where the Russian prostitutes were at odds with the African women.

"Even the Negro women fear the Russians, because Russian people are the nastiest."

The middle-aged women were afraid they would earn nothing if they were forced to pay taxes. "If there were taxes," one of them said, "we would have to work even harder to support ourselves and our families." In effect, the state would take on the role of pimp.

One older woman was indignant about an official who, during a TV interview, had proposed legalizing prostitution and using the monies earned to build roads.

> "We can barely suck enough cock to buy kasha, and now they want us to pay for the roads."

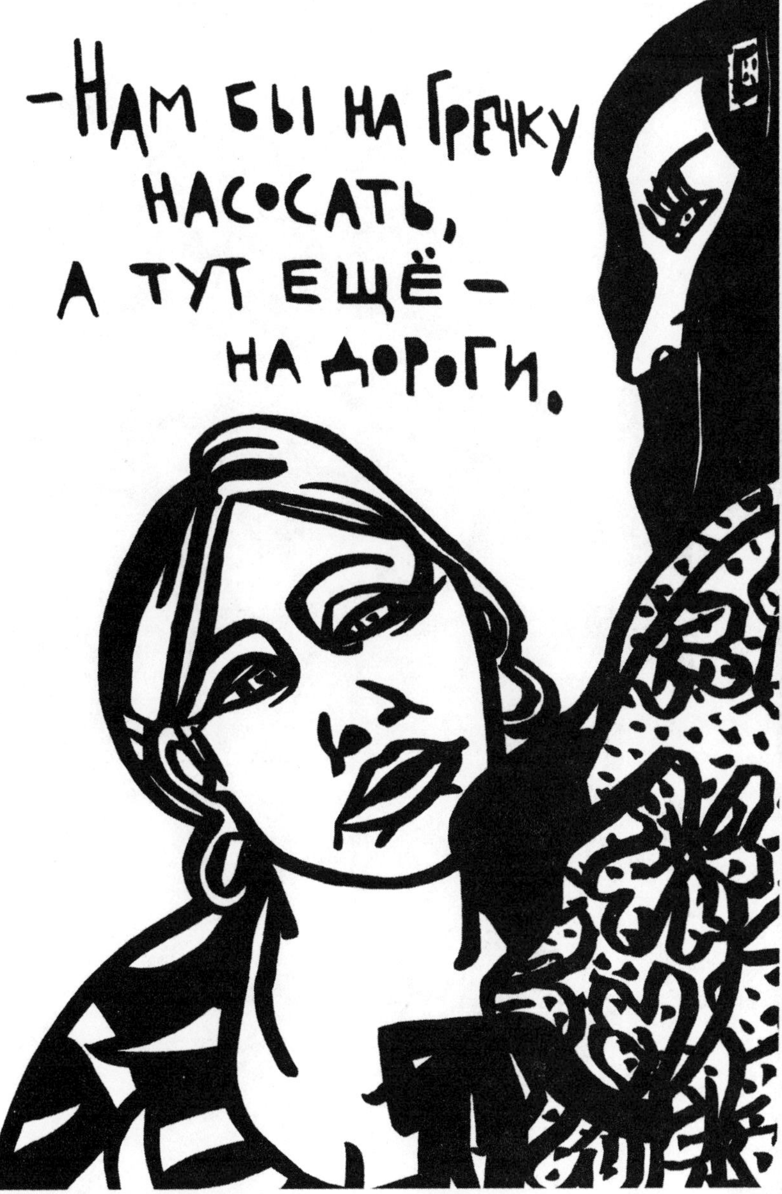
—НАМ БЫ НА ГРЕЧКУ НАСОСАТЬ, А ТУТ ЕЩЁ — НА ДОРОГИ.

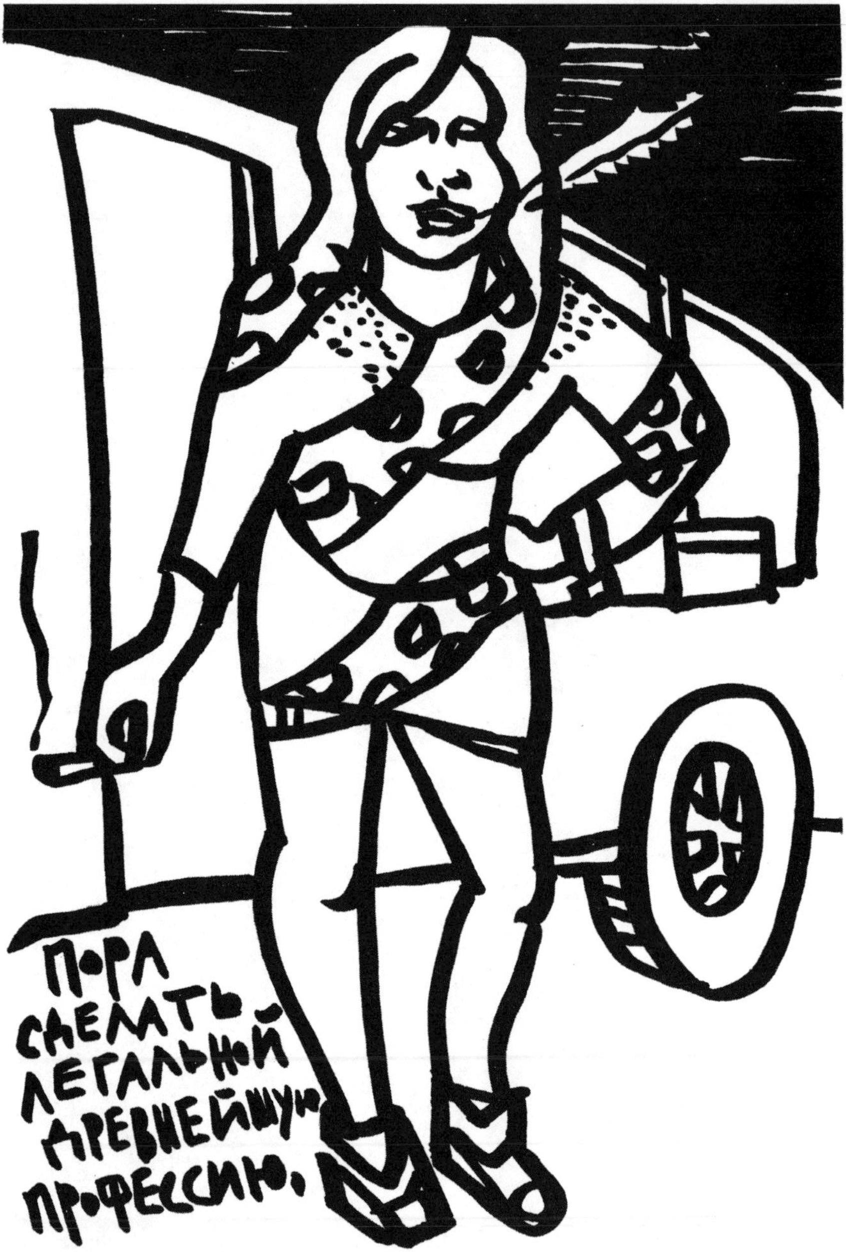
ПОРА
СДЕЛАТЬ
ЛЕГАЛЬНОЙ
ДРЕВНЕЙШУЮ
ПРОФЕССИЮ.

"It's the cops who make legalization necessary."

The working girls at all the offices I visited agreed on this point. Policemen arrange "unpaid work days" where they force the girls to service them for free.

And it's much tougher in the capital. Girls who had been "on tour" in Moscow told me what it was like. "In Moscow, cops patrol the street lineups and take a cut from each client. So the women have to service more clients to make money." One girl came back from a "tour" with a scar.

"Officials are against legalization, but all of them are our clients," the girls said sardonically. "Many officials run their own offices under the guise of massage parlors."

"It's time to make the world's oldest profession legal."

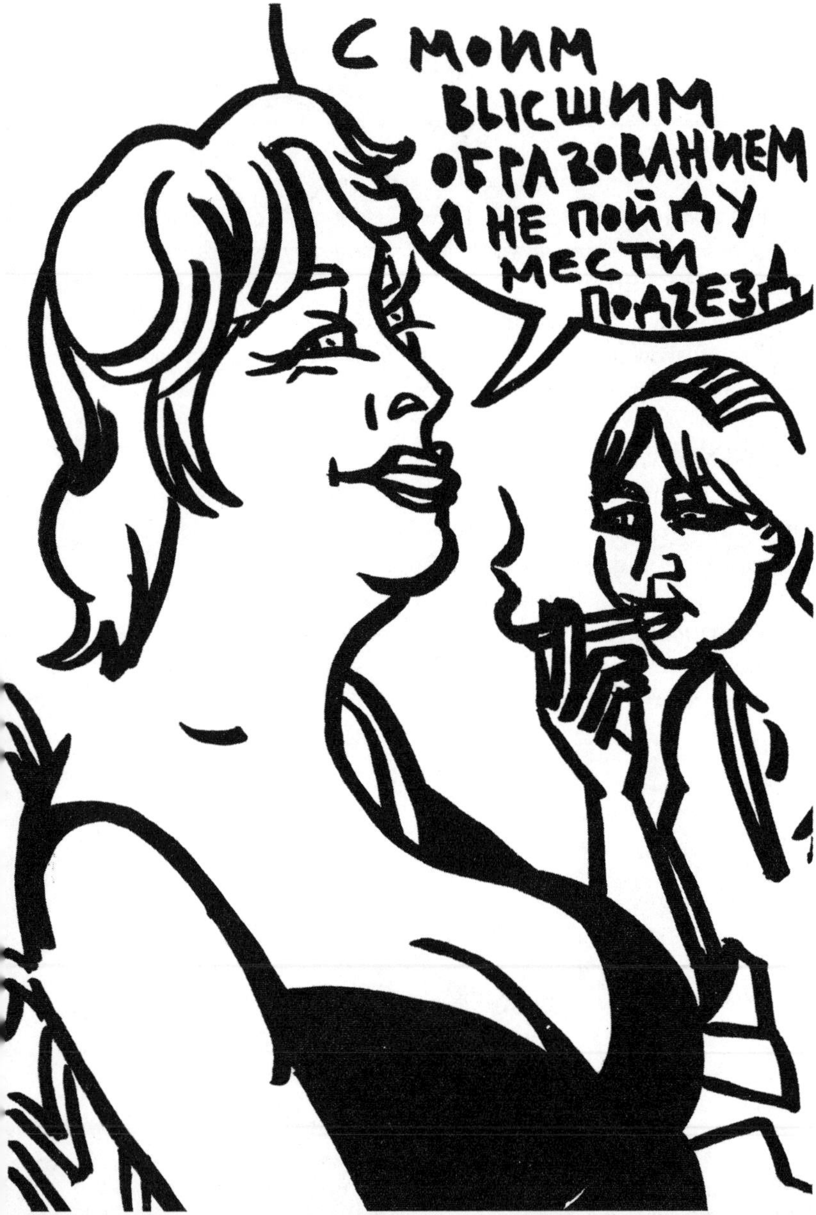
С МОИМ ВЫСШИМ ОБРАЗОВАНИЕМ Я НЕ ПОЙДУ МЕСТИ ПОДЪЕЗД

This older woman was 55. She also worked a legitimate job and was glad she could retire with a pension. Not all the so-called dames have a pension to look forward to. Women whose sole source of income has been sex work will get low-skilled jobs as shop clerks, cleaners, and so on to make ends meet. Many of the women in their forties fear the day when clients stop asking for them.

The younger working girls wonder where they would go, given their lack of higher education. The older women, who were educated in the Soviet era but do not have decent salaries, consider "dirty" work dirtier than prostitution.

Both groups of women were firm about the fact that what they did was a "normal" job. And both groups agreed that if other decently paid work were available, they would not stay in prostitution.

"I have a college degree. I'm not about to sweep stairwells."

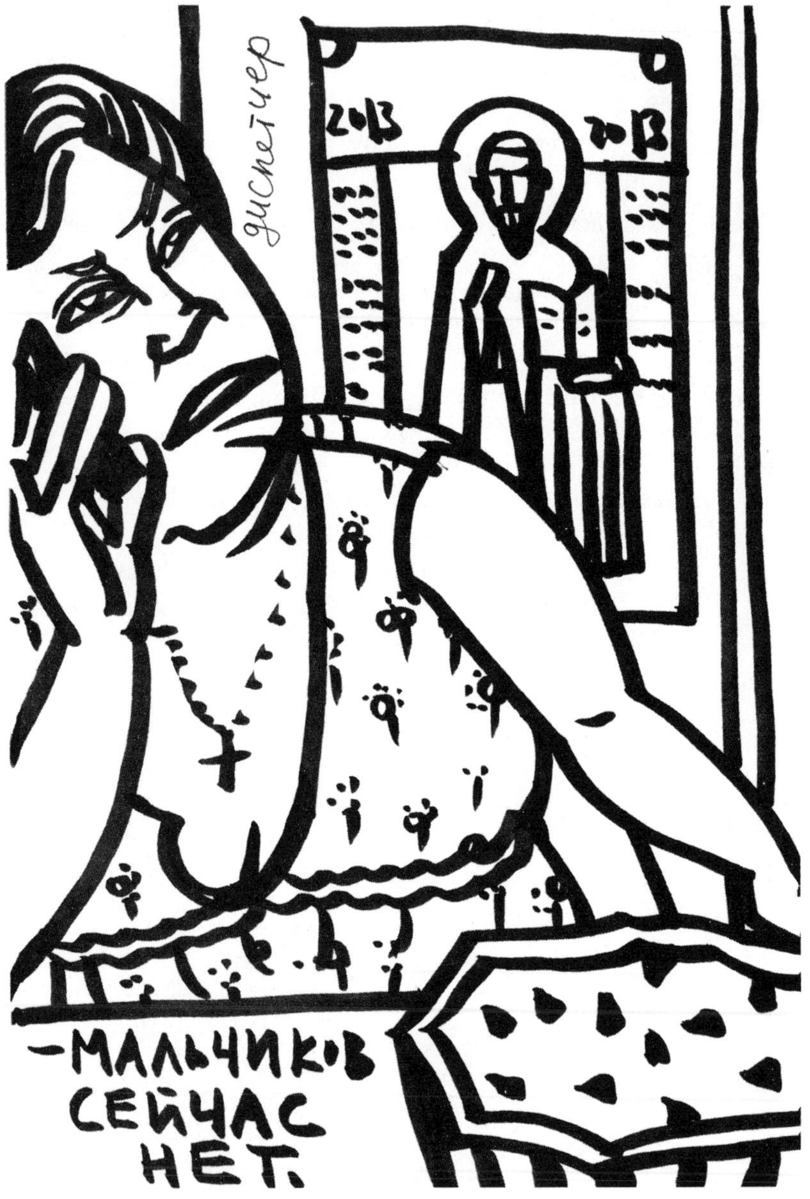
диспетчер
— МАЛЬЧИКОВ СЕЙЧАС НЕТ.

This was an office run by a former factory worker, a 60-year-old woman with diabetes. She had turned a room in her apartment into chambers, and herself into a dispatcher. Her daughters had once had to work as prostitutes to earn money for the family, but they had called it quits: what their mother now earned was enough for everyone. The daughters got married, and the factory-worker-turned-dispatcher had recently become a grandmother for the fifth time. She sympathized with all the working girls, especially the ones who "survived only due to sanitary wet wipes." She told me about a girl who had recently died. She had long been ill with pneumonia, but had kept working anyway.

DISPATCHER: "We don't have any boys at the moment."

—Пока клиентов нет, спим в машине.

Call girls—girls without their own chambers or offices—work out of cars and vans. I spent time in one such minivan. Four girls sat crowded together on the seat opposite me. While they waited for clients to call, they drank wine from a box and beer from cans, the rhinestones on their outfits and their gorgeously painted eyes glittering. They were very different from the "office" girls. They reminded me of pilots, ready at any moment to parachute out of the cockpit. They had the special charisma of people for whom the risk of death has become commonplace. One girl's face was crisscrossed by a scar. Working on call is more dangerous than working in an office because it's harder to protect yourself from infection and violent clients. But it's even more dangerous to work on the street, in a lineup. The girls who work lineups are mostly heroin addicts who would not be hired to work in offices. They are often also infected with syphilis, hepatitis, and HIV. But clients stop for them anyway, even clients in expensive cars. I suspect they are attracted by the extent of these women's personal degradation, which makes it easier to treat them like objects.

"When there are no customers, we sleep in the car."

"All morning I prayed to God that the rain wouldn't ruin my sign."
SIGN: *KARL MARX, FRIEDRICH ENGELS, VLADIMIR LENIN*

ANGRY

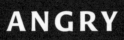

LENIN

KAPITALINA IVANONVA:
"Lenin lives! It's what I live for!"

WHAT A TALENT FOR TREATING
THE PEOPLE LIKE IDIOTS

VALENTINA, 73 YEARS OLD: "Way to
go, Pussy Riot! I would have sung 'Mother
of God, Drive Putin Away' with them."

PUSSY RIOT SOLIDARITY BLOC, MARCH OF MILLIONS, MOSCOW, MAY 6, 2012

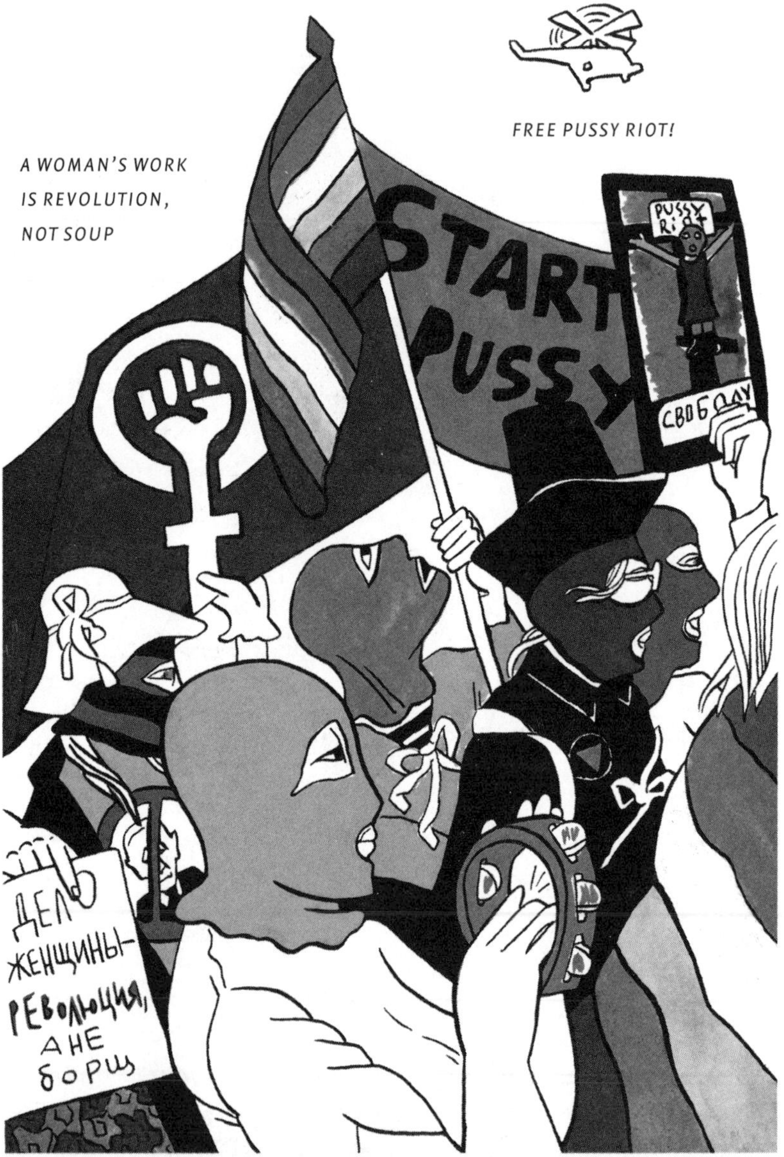
START PUSSY
PUSSY RIOT
СВОБОДУ
ДЕЛ
ЖЕНЩИНЫ-
РЕВОЛЮЦИЯ,
А НЕ
БОРЩ

A WOMAN'S WORK IS REVOLUTION, NOT SOUP

FREE PUSSY RIOT!

NATIONALIST BLOC, MARCH OF MILLIONS 3,
MOSCOW, SEPTEMBER 15, 2012

"Put Pussy Riot in the trash!"

GLORY TO RUSSIA!
LOVE ONE ANOTHER

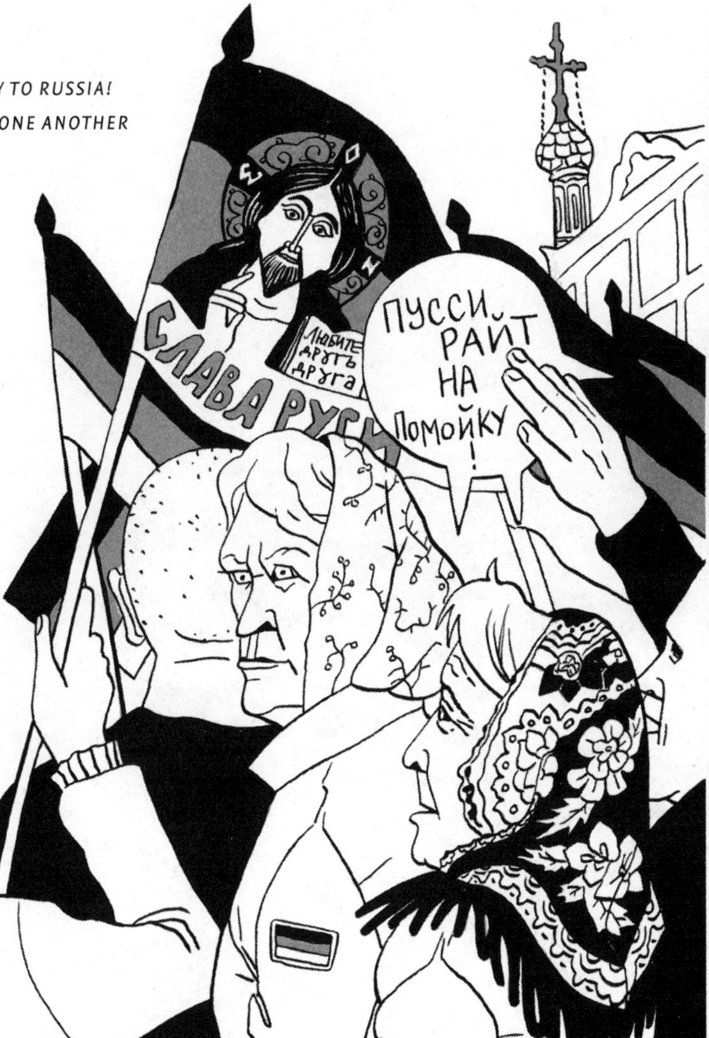
СЛАВА РУСИ
ЛЮБИТЕ ДРУГЪ ДРУГА
ПУССИ РАЙТ НА ПОМОЙКУ!

A CHRONICLE OF RESISTANCE

In late 2011, for the first time since the early 1990s, heavily attended protest rallies took place in Moscow. The possibility of an Orange Revolution was discussed in the press. Many artists were involved in the protests. They staged actions and outdoor exhibitions, did the decorations for rallies, and put out samizdat publications. But the most powerful action of all was Pussy Riot's performance at Christ the Savior Cathedral.

Beginning with the Russian State Duma elections (on December 4, 2011), I kept a "chronicle of resistance" in which I made on-the-spot sketches of all the important protest-related events I witnessed. I wanted to make a portrait of each rally and to show how the protests changed—to single out the highlights, capture new characters, and document the direct speech of the people involved.

DECEMBER 4, 2011

On election day, I worked as a sketch artist/reporter in Khimki, on the edge of Moscow. At my polling station, journalists and all observers, except those from the ruling United Russia party, were removed under various pretexts, but I, the female artist, was allowed to stay on as an amusing oddity. I witnessed one bus after another bringing people who voted with absentee ballots. They were mainly from various factories and, quite often, from other towns. The drivers shouted at them to vote faster because they had to ferry them to the next polling station.

Ordinary residents who had come to vote on their own were unable to get through to the table where ballots were issued. By evening, and in the days to come, the internet was busy with photos and videos documenting election fraud and observers wrote about gross violations. Coupled with Putin's decision to become president again, this evidence undermined any illusions about civil liberties in Russia—and any hopes for change.

UNITED RUSSIA ELECTION OBSERVER

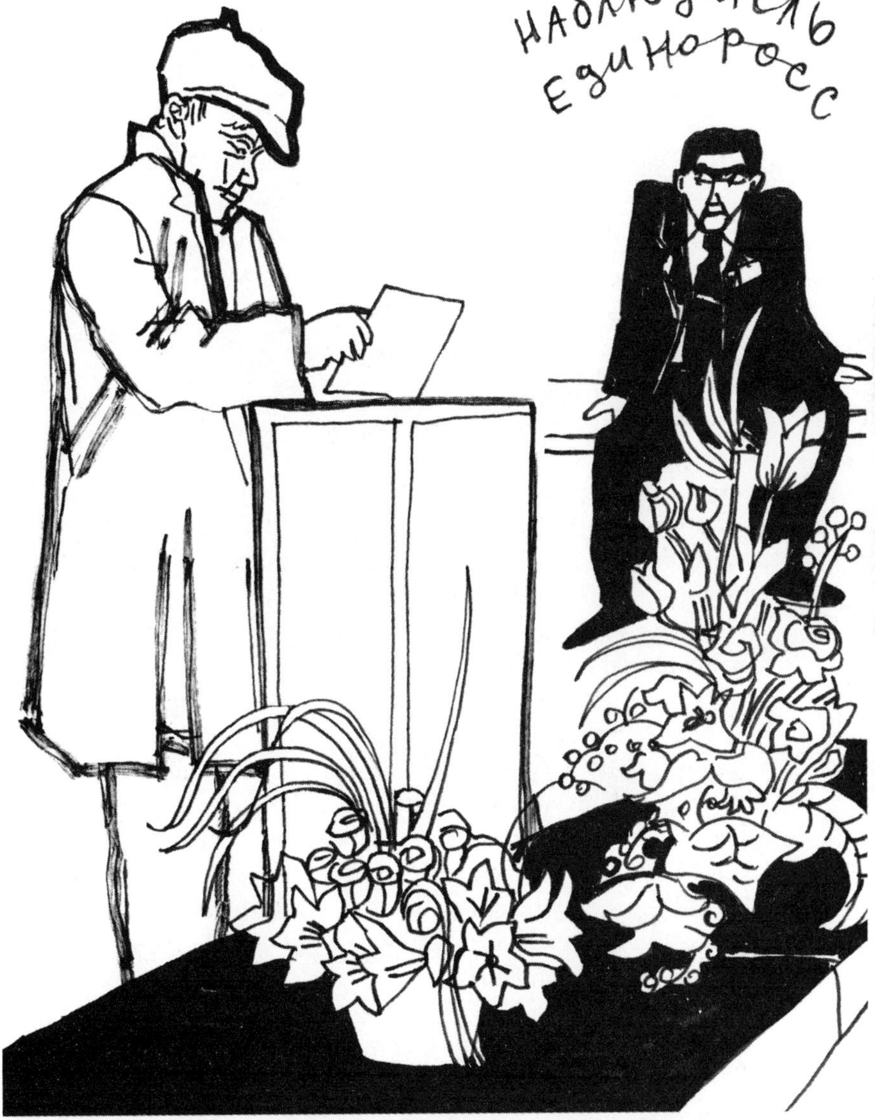
Наблюдатель
единоросс

WOMEN TALKING ON PHONE: "We're yelling at an opposition rally.
We have to yell for another two hours."
MAN WITH MEGAPHONE: "Russia! Putin! Medvedev!

I missed the December 5 rally at Chistye Prudy. The same evening,
protesters organized an event through social media: a rally on
December 6 on Triumfalnaya Square. Launched by Eduard
Limonov, protests in defense of the freedom of assembly had been
taking place on Triumfalnaya since 2009. Although the authorities did not sanction the December 6 rally, thousands of people
gathered for it anyway. At the subway exit, protesters were greeted
by people from the pro-Putin youth organization Nashi, who were
pounding on drums, and battalions of police in so-called diving
suits—heavy body armor and helmets. Police roughed up protesters when they detained them. Plainclothes security services
officers and Nashi members videotaped the proceedings from the
other side of the barriers. I stood next to them; I was taken for
a Nashi member and praised for my talent. I drew in the speech
bubbles afterwards, at home.

News of the arrests on Triumfalnaya only fueled people's desire to protest. On Facebook, approximately 40,000 people said they would attend a "Rally for Honest Elections." Revolution Square was the designated meeting place. On the internet, in kitchens and offices, people discussed the possibility of revolution and the likelihood that the demonstration would be dispersed by force of arms. Liberal leaders (Boris Nemtsov, Sergei Parkhomenko, and Vladimir Ryzhkov) made a deal with the authorities that the rally would be permitted if the protesters were moved to Bolotnaya Square and away from the Kremlin.

WE'RE FUCKING SICK OF THEM

WOMAN HOLDING FLOWERS: "Are the police with the people?"

The opposition rally on December 10 was attended by tens of thousands of people—the first opposition rally of that size since the early 1990s. The police did not detain anyone. I think that many people were so excited to be in the throng of the 100,000-strong demonstration—and so impressed by the beauty of marching under multicolored flags—that they stopped critically evaluating what was happening.

MAN TALKING ON PHONE: "All of Moscow is here."
SIGN AT LEFT: *UNITED RUSSIA SHOULD BE ASHAMED*
SIGN ON BALLOONS: *RETIRE PUTIN*

The December 24 rally on Sakharov Avenue was memorable because of the clear presence of the "common people"—a crowd of people who were poorly dressed, didn't have iPhones, and didn't have any party allegiances. The "people" took to the streets without creative signs, and they used foul language when they commented on the speeches made by socialite and media celebrity Ksenia Sobchak and Putin's ex-finance minister Alexei Kudrin.

CROWD: "We beat Hitler, we'll beat Putin!"
LARGE BANNER: *DOWN WITH PRESIDENTIAL AUTOCRACY!*

On a frosty afternoon, the so-called March for Fair Elections proceeded from Bolshaya Yakimanka Street to Bolotnaya Square in four columns—liberals, right-wingers, leftists, and a non-aligned "civic" column.

On February 15, Taisiya Osipova appealed her sentence in the regional court in Smolensk, in western Russia. Osipova, an activist with the unregistered political party Other Russia, had been convicted, in December 2011, of selling heroin and sentenced to ten years in prison. The artist and the Other Russia party activist Matvei "Skif" Krylov organized a Free Taisiya Osipova auto rally from Moscow to Smolensk. On the night of February 14, around sixty activists, including me, set out for Smolensk to show our support for Osipova, who we believed was framed, and whom we thus regarded as a political prisoner. The entire way there, we were followed by a jeep full of plainclothes officers from Center "E," the special "anti-extremism" police formed during Dmitry Medvedev's term as president.

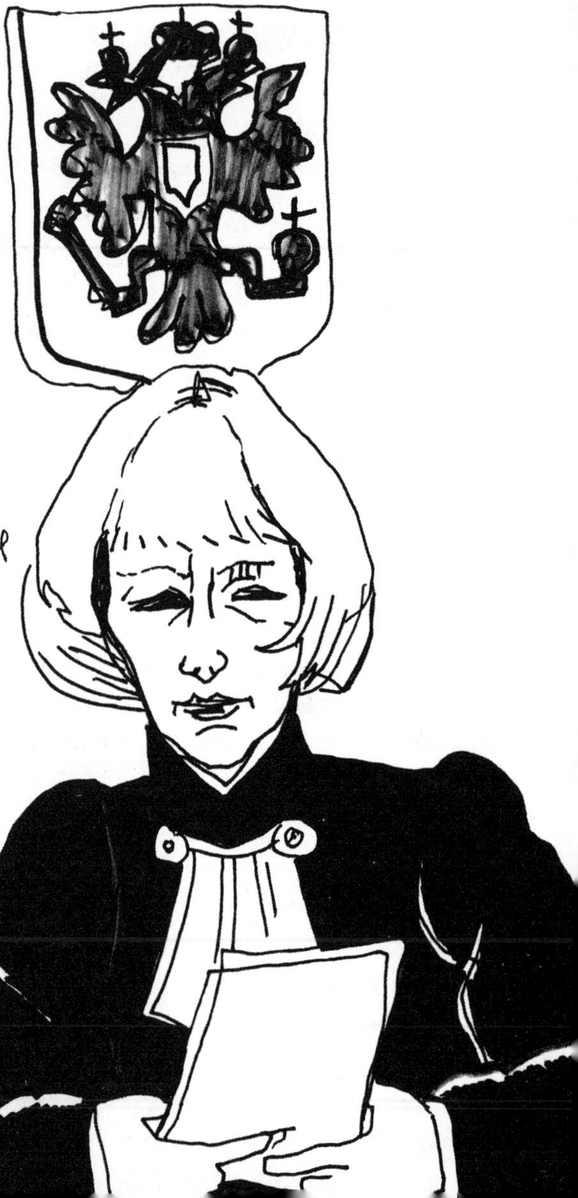

Приговор отменён.
Дело возвращается
в районный суд
на новое
рассмотрение.
Осипова
остаётся
под арестом
до
15
марта.

JUDGE: "The verdict is overturned, and the case will be sent back to the district court for retrial. Osipova will remain in police custody until March 15."

At the appeals hearing, the prosecutor unexpectedly asked the court to sentence Osipova to four years in prison instead of the original ten, but then the judge reversed the verdict altogether and sent the case back to a lower court for a retrial. The activists shared their feelings with each other—their joy was mixed with fear that the reprisal against Osipova had been postponed until Putin's victory in the upcoming presidential elections. On August 28, 2012, Osipova was sentenced to eight years in prison. The court was unmoved by the fact that she is a diabetic (a death sentence, given the conditions in Russian prisons) and that she has a young daughter.

The grassroots White Circle flash mob resembled an unwitting reprise of the 2007 performance "White Line," when artists from the Trade Union of Street Art drew a white chalk line around Moscow's inner Garden Ring. During White Circle, protesters sporting white symbols—white clothes, white balloons, white flowers, white toys, white dogs—joined hands along the entire length of the Garden Ring. White ribbons waved from passing cars, the snow was falling, and the mood was upbeat. The only thing spoiling it were Nashi members holding signs that read, "Only 8 days left until Putin's victory."

НАБЛЮДАТЕЛИ
НАБЛЮДАЮТ
ЗА ПОДСЧЁТОМ
ГОЛОСОВ

ELECTION OBSERVERS OBSERVING THE VOTE COUNT

Thousands of activist observers worked the presidential election. I was part of a mobile group organized by the Citizen Observer project. Shuttling between polling stations, we saw rows of buses from Belgorod, Vladimir, Saratov, and other towns. At the polling stations themselves, we saw long lines of provincial workers and students bearing absentee ballots. In the evening, they were treated to a festive concert on Manezh Square.

Despite the fact that all opposition forces were mobilized in the capital, Putin officially mustered 48.25% of the vote in Moscow, and 63.6% nationwide.

"We will begin carrying out peaceful acts of civil disobedience."

Pushkin Square was the site of another Fair Elections rally the following day. There were fewer creative signs and more anger as people shared their impressions of the election. We stood in the cold, knee-deep in snow under a full moon. Leftist leader Sergei Udaltsov urged protesters not to go home "until Putin leaves." Police dispersed the several hundred people who heeded his call and stayed. Many of them were sentenced to fifteen days in jail.

SIGN AT LEFT: *PUTIN IS AN OUTLAW*

SIGN AT RIGHT: *REVOLUTION*

WOMAN IN PARKA: "People where I work were forced to vote for Putin."

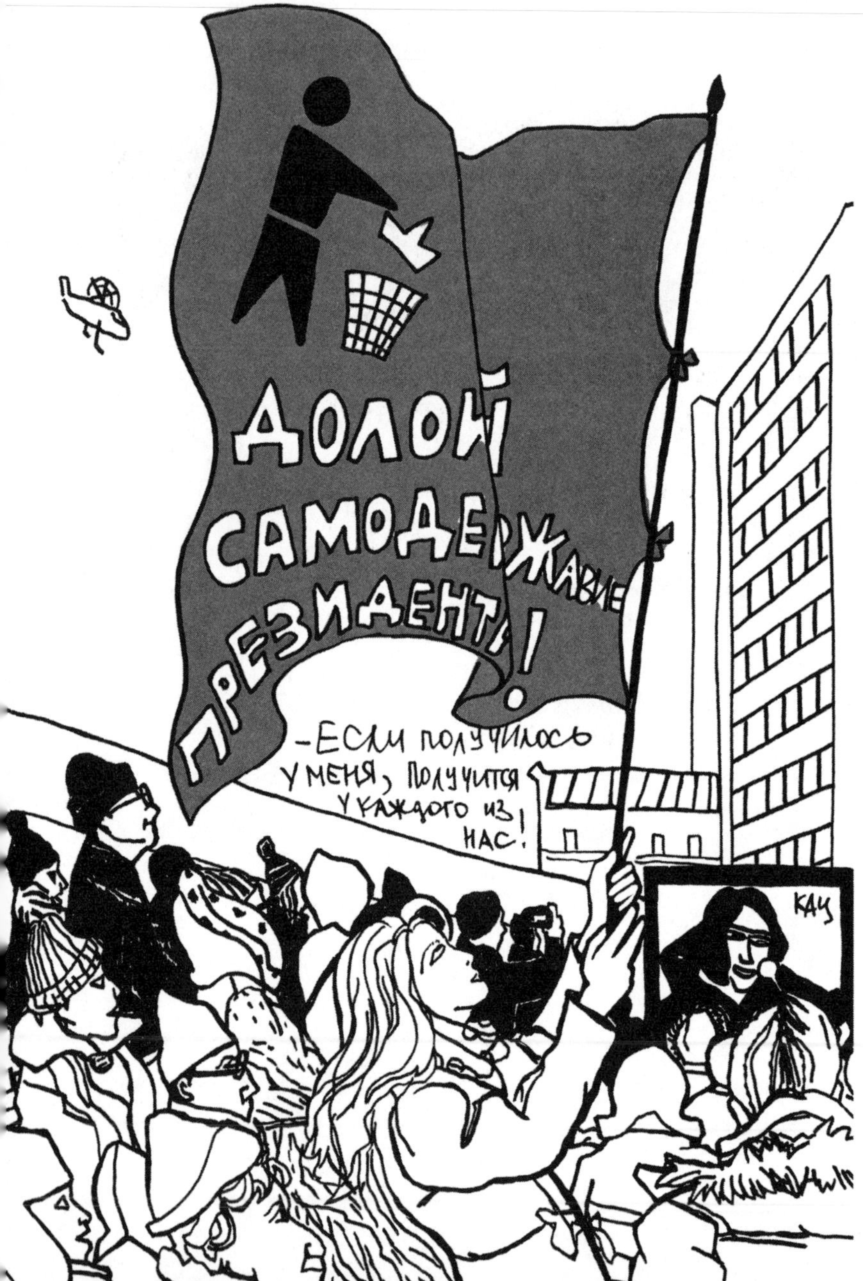
ДОЛОЙ САМОДЕРЖАВИЕ ПРЕЗИДЕНТА!
–ЕСЛИ ПОЛУЧИЛОСЬ У МЕНЯ, ПОЛУЧИТСЯ У КАЖДОГО ИЗ НАС!
КАЦ

MARCH 10, 2012

SLOGAN ON FLAG: *DOWN WITH THE PRESIDENT'S AUTOCRACY!*
MAXIM KATZ: "If I can do it, every one of us can!"

The last Fair Elections rally took place on New Arbat Street in Moscow. Maxim Katz and other victors in municipal district council elections urged the crowd not to despair and to shift their focus to addressing social issues. Speakers mentioned the political prisoners from Pussy Riot, and the first signs I'd seen supporting the group were scattered amidst the crowd. The next protest was scheduled for May 6.

In between the thousands-strong Fair Elections rallies, so-called Pussy Riot Court Festivals were held outside courthouses where hearings in the case took place. Artists were heavily involved in these protests, producing leaflets and signs, and organizing performances.

On April 19, the three accused members of Pussy Riot were brought to their pretrial custody hearing from the pretrial detention facility where they had been held since their arrest. During the breaks in the hearing, Nadya Tolokonnikova complained of constant headaches and spoke out harshly against Putin. Katya Samutsevich refused to give interviews, saying that one had to be careful with information about Pussy Riot. Masha Alyokhina comforted her loved ones ("I have no problems in prison") and quoted the poet Osip Mandelstam.

NADYA TOLOKONNIKOVA: "I wish the people who put us here a life in prison like ours."

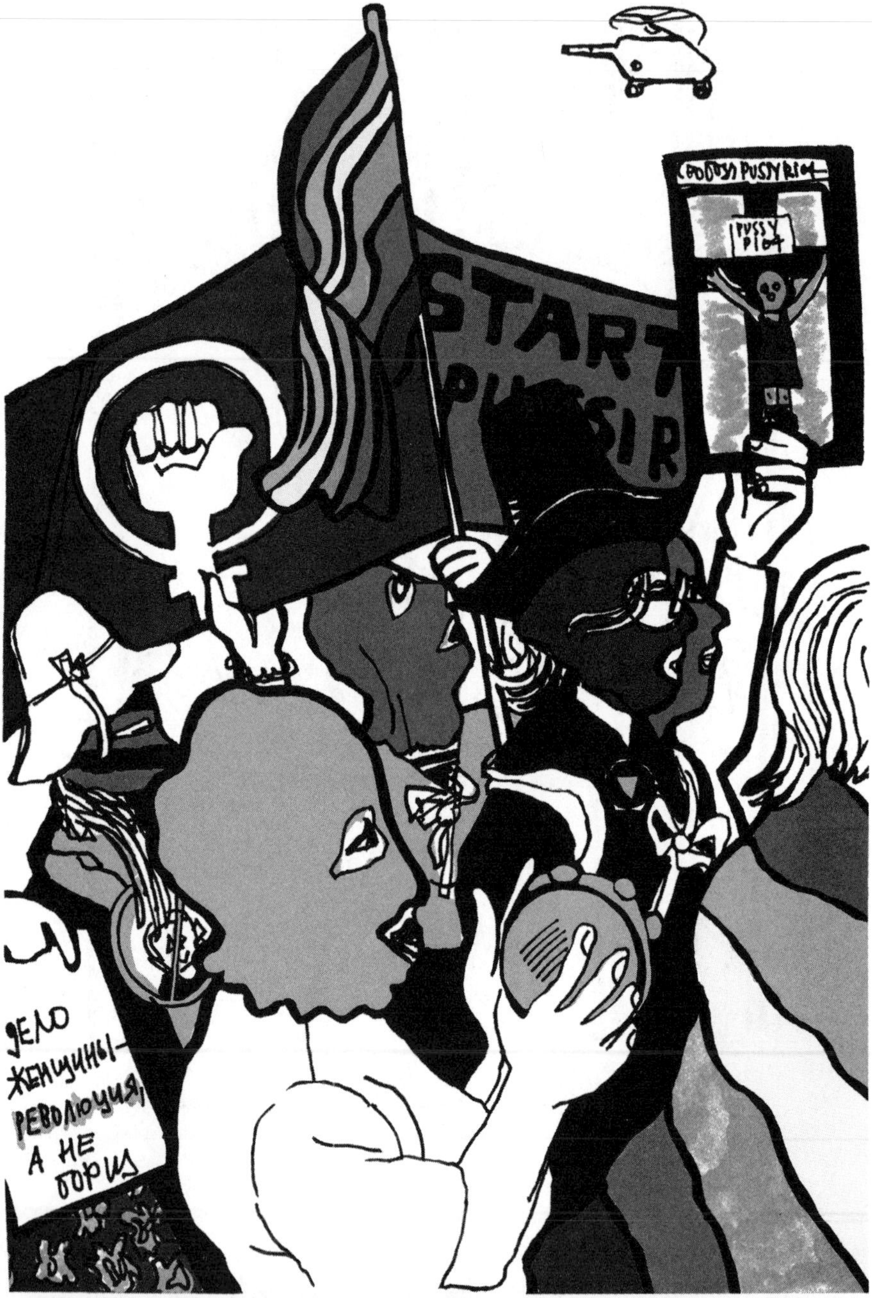
START
СВОБОДУ PUSSY RIOT
PUSSY RIOT
ДЕЛО
ЖЕНЩИНЫ—
РЕВОЛЮЦИЯ,
А НЕ
БОРЩ

MAY 6, 2012

Despite the start of the summer dacha season, around 50,000 people gathered for the so-called March of Millions. Many people were glad to see an LGBT rainbow column at the march, which carried signs and banners in support of Pussy Riot. When the marchers arrived at Bolotnaya Square, the police blocked their way. It was not clear what was happening.

WOMAN AT LEFT: "I'm trying to dissuade my husband from emigrating—I want to raise our kids here."
HER SIGN: *IT'S IMPORTANT TO BELIEVE IN A HAPPY FUTURE*
WOMAN AT RIGHT: "I want to live in Russia."
HER SIGN: *OUR HEARTS HAVE ALREADY CHANGED*

Suddenly, the police began to disperse people by swinging billy clubs and spraying tear gas. Police hit a young man over the head right in front of me, and he fell to the ground bleeding. "They murdered him! They murdered him!" women wailed. Several protesters overturned portable toilets, and the shit from them flowed over the policemen's feet. The police divided protesters into groups, drove them through the streets, and beat and detained them, but they were unable to force people to leave the area between Bolotnaya Square and the Tretyakov Gallery until nightfall. Later, I learned that the authorities had changed the route of the march without warning, and a sit-in by protesters to challenge this had led the police to attack.

Immediately after the events of May 6, the Russian Federation's Investigative Committee launched an investigation into the so-called riots and alleged cases of violence against police officers. Moscow City Court is currently hearing the trial of twelve rank-and-file march participants. Two defendants in the case have already been sentenced to two and a half and four and a half years in prison, respectively. One of the May 6 prisoners, Mikhail Kosenko, faces compulsory psychiatric treatment.

WOMAN: "Why are there riot police everywhere?"
POLICEMAN: "Because of the folk celebrations."

Putin was reinaugurated as president on May 7, so disgruntled citizens began holding round-the-clock "folk celebrations" in downtown Moscow as a way of protesting without obtaining permission from the authorities. Two downtown subway stations, Arbatskaya and Kropotkinskaya, which the newly elected president's motorcade would pass, were closed "for security reasons." All streets and alleys leading to the Kremlin were cordoned off by the police early in the morning and cleared of people. Police dispersed people involved in the folk celebrations, too. People caught wearing white ribbons, a symbol of the opposition, were arrested immediately.

MAY 9, 2012, PUSHKIN SQUARE

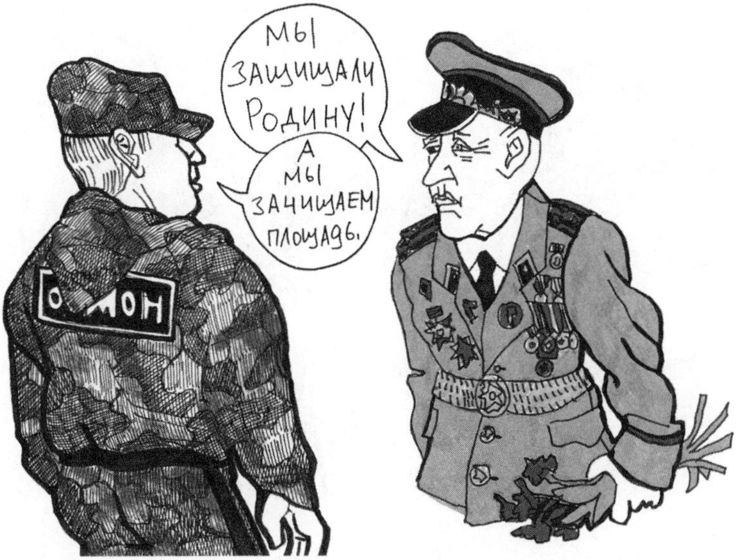
Мы защищали Родину!
А мы зачищаем площадь.
ОМОН

VETERAN: "We defended the Motherland!"
RIOT COP: "And we are mopping up the square."

May 9, 2012, felt more like Police Occupation Day than Victory Day. There were even more police, military vehicles, and metal barriers than on May 7.

By midday, the opposition—mainly protesters from the folk celebrations—had begun closing ranks at Chistye Prudy. In the evening, paddy wagons appeared on both sides of Chistoprudny Boulevard, but for some reason the police did not disperse the 1,500 activists. Despite the threat of arrest, at least 100 people spent the night at Chistye Prudy by the monument to the Kazakh poet Abay Kunanbayev.

LECTURE ON CIVIL DISOBEDIENCE

The Occupy Abay camp took shape at Chistye Prudy the next morning. More and more activists kept coming. They brought foam pads, sleeping bags, food, guitars, and samizdat publications. People talked enthusiastically with one another and sang lots of Viktor Tsoi songs. I moved about the camp amidst the dense crowd, wondering how I could convey in pictures the meaning and mood of this ferment on Chistoprudny Boulevard. When it got dark, the free people's kitchen, faintly illuminated by street lamps, was somehow reminiscent of the Last Supper.

The core Occupy Abay activists almost never left the camp while it was running. They slept on the ground in sleeping bags. Left Front activists, anarchists, LGBT people, and nationalists took joint responsibility for cleaning the camp, running the people's kitchen, and maintaining order. Rank-and-file members of the protest movement also tried to spend as much time as possible in the camp: many of them blew off classes or took time off from work. There were daily free lectures on political and social issues, and people discussed the future of the protest movement. Occupy Abay was crowded even when it was cold and rainy. Everyone regarded its existence as a miracle.

At five in the morning on May 16, the police dispersed Occupy Abay. The pretext was a complaint filed in the Basmanny District Court by several residents of 9 Chistoprudny Boulevard, who complained of "noise, filth and trampled lawns." Occupy moved to Barrikadnaya, but it proved impossible to organize a kitchen and sleeping area at the new location and thus live in the camp around the clock. Most activists came only in the evening for the general assemblies, during which further plans were discussed. Everyone could express their opinion, and decisions were voted on collectively.

MAN: "Six months ago, I left my business to take part in the protests with my girlfriend."

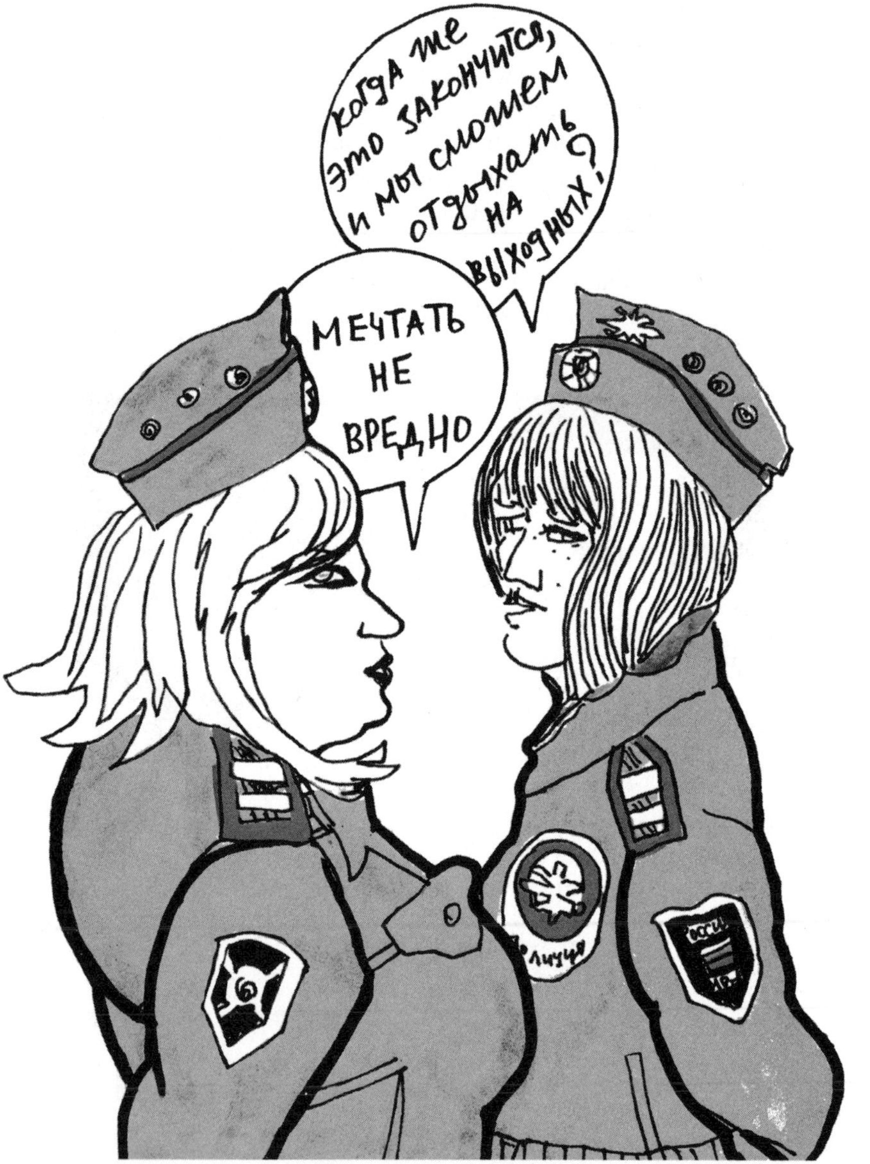
когда же это закончится, и мы сможем отдыхать на выходных?
МЕЧТАТЬ НЕ ВРЕДНО

MAY 18, 2012, KUDRINSKAYA SQUARE

POLICEWOMAN AT RIGHT: "When is this going to end so we can get weekends off?"
POLICEWOMAN AT LEFT: "It doesn't hurt to dream."

You could still sense popular unity at Occupy Barrikadnaya. I remember a young woman who would come with shopping bags stuffed with sandwiches to feed the hungry activists. Her sandwich gave me the strength to continue drawing for another couple of hours. Another time, it started to rain, and a group of nationalists gave me a raincoat. It was the police who poisoned life in the Occupy camp: they detained people, stole food, and at one point, they seized the donations box for the camp. On May 19, the police dispersed Occupy Barrikadnaya. There were attempts to reestablish the camp in the days that followed, but each time they were thwarted by the police. Some protesters relocated to Old Orbat, where Occupy degenerated into street gatherings involving peaceful songs accompanied by guitar, flirting, and idle chitchat about various topics.

"Antifa!"

"The antifa are fags!"

The second so-called March of Millions started on Pushkin Square. Columns of anarchists and nationalists marched on opposite sides of the Boulevard Ring, the neo-Nazis shouting insults at the antifa. The research and education column came out for the first time: its members protested new laws aimed at dismantling the education system. The march ended on Sakharov Avenue. Police estimated that 18,000 people attended the event, while organizers put the number at around 100,000.

PUSSY RIOT: "This trial reflects the will of one person."

The Khamovniki District Court began hearing the Pussy Riot case on July 30. I was able to attend the fifth and sixth hearings. Hundreds of journalists covered the trial, and the hearings were broadcast live, so my drawings played no special role in the general media flow. I was just fascinated by the chance to sketch this historic trial.

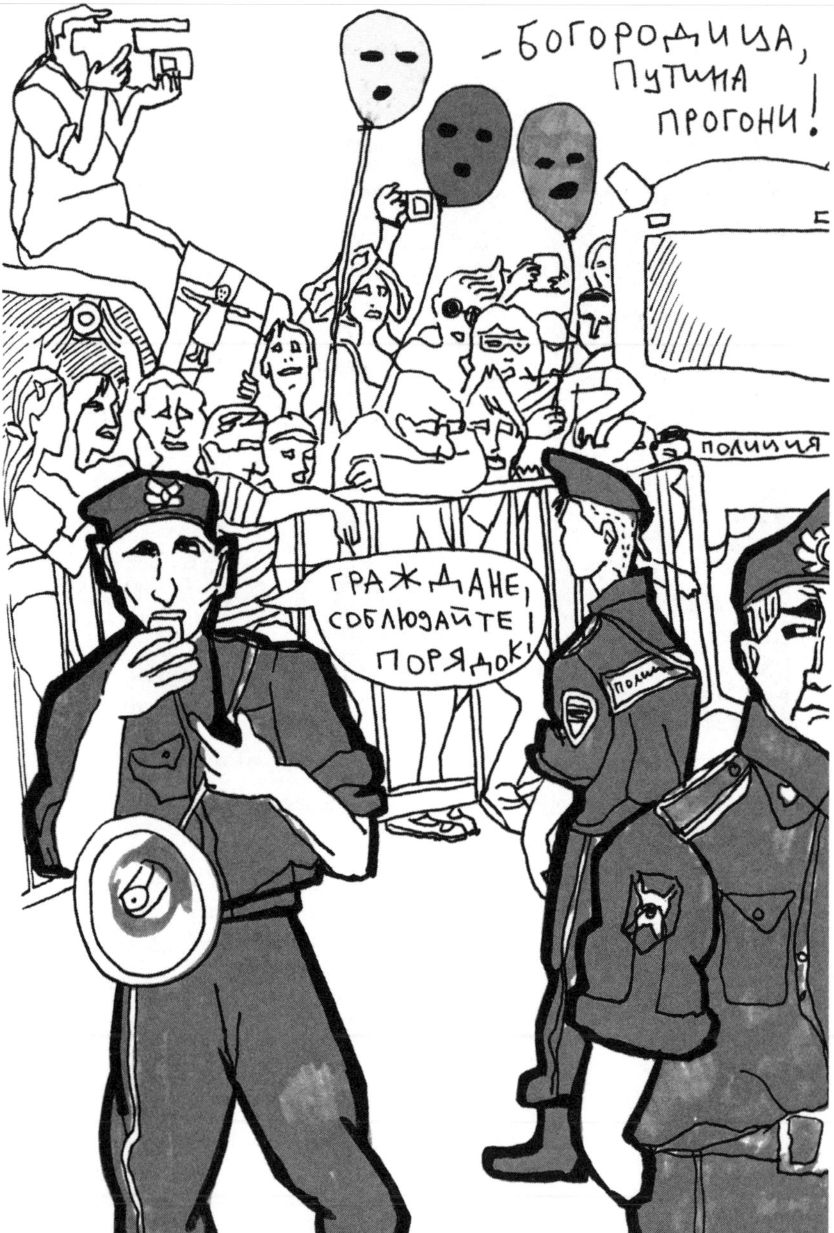
- БОГОРОДИЦА, ПУТИНА ПРОГОНИ!
ПОЛИЦИЯ
ГРАЖДАНЕ, СОБЛЮДАЙТЕ ПОРЯДОК!

AUGUST 17, 2012

POLICEMAN: "Citizens, keep the peace!"
CROWD: "Mother of God, drive Putin away!"

The verdict in the Pussy Riot trial was read in Moscow's Khamovniki District Court on August 17. Nadya Tolokonnikova, Masha Alyokhina, and Katya Samutsevich were each sentenced to two years in prison. A spontaneous demonstration began when hundreds of the punk group's supporters surrounded the courthouse. Police snatched people from the crowd—teenagers in colored balaclavas, old women with signs, prominent opposition figures—and threw them into paddy wagons. Tolokonnikova was sent to a prison in Mordovia, while Alyokhina initially served her sentence near Perm. During an appeals hearing on October 10, Samutsevich was released on probation, allegedly because during the punk prayer she had been unable to climb over the railing and dance on the altar with the other women.

NATIONALISTS: "Moscow without darkies!"

After the summer lull, the third March of Millions, the least well attended, took place. It repeated the route of the previous march. A fight broke out between the nationalists and the anti-fascists. People in the communist column blamed liberals for the petering out of protests. Liberals expressed their fear of both the rightists and leftists. The event was scheduled to last until ten in the evening, but by five o'clock people had gone home. Sergei Udaltsov urged the hundred or so protesters who remained to organize a maidan or veche (popular assembly). He was arrested at 10:01 PM.

PUSSY RIOT

"Free the prisoners! Shame on the Russian Orthodox Church!"

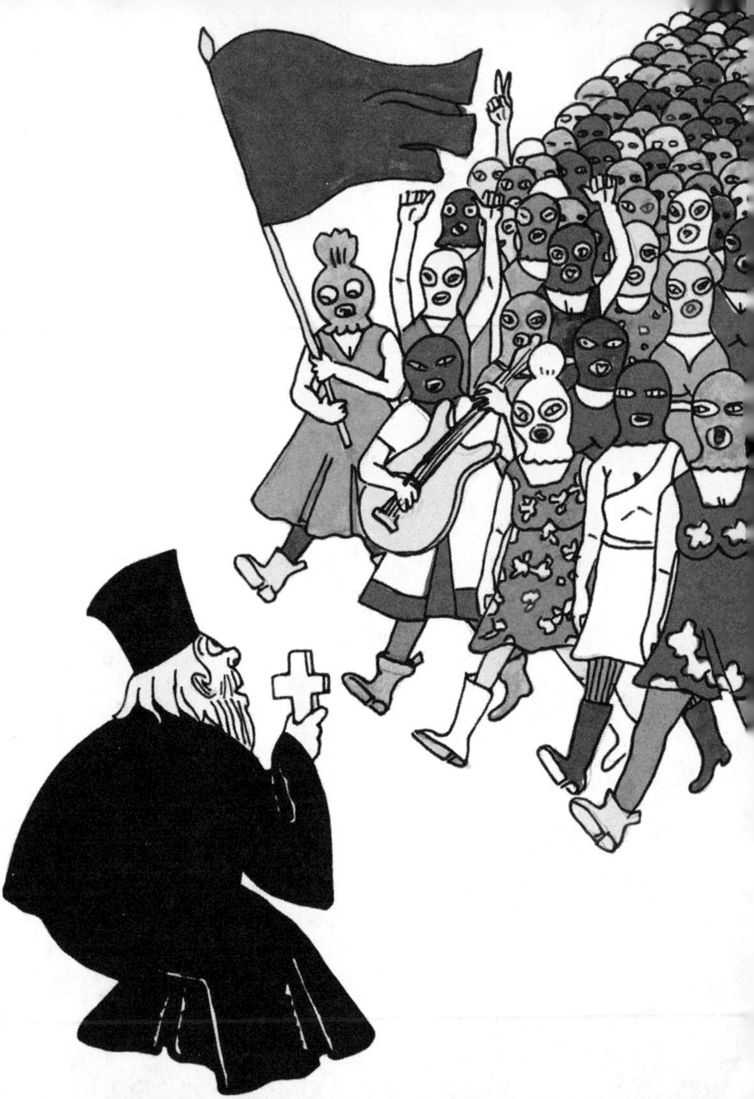

PUSSY RIOT PRETRIAL HEARING, TAGANSKY DISTRICT COURT, MOSCOW, APRIL 19, 2012

Because of the huge number of journalists on hand, the pretrial hearing was delayed for over an hour as police cleared a path to the courtroom cage for the accused and their armed escort guard.

KATYA SAMUTSEVICH'S FATHER

Следователь
сказал, это
не обязан мне объяснеть
отказ в свиданиех
с дочерью

Наталье Сергеевна Алехина

NATALYA ALYOKHINA: "The investigator said he wasn't obligated to explain to me why my requests to visit my daughter have been turned down."

Masha Alyokhina's mother had not seen her daughter since February.

NADYA TOLOKONNIKOVA: "I wish the people who put us here a life in prison like ours."

Nadya Tolokonnikova's case was the first to be heard.

Tolokonnikova gave a five-minute statement to the courtroom gallery.

Afterwards, she chatted for a few minutes with her husband, Pyotr Verzilov, and with journalists, many of them her friends.

These were the highlights of Tolokonnikova's statement:

> Our performance was directed against the fusion of church and state.
> In jail, Patriarch Kirill is always shown on Channel One. In fact, he is on more often than President Bear Cub (i.e., Medvedev).
> When you're in jail, the only interesting thing is the fact Putin has hijacked the country.
> Prison is a not a bad place for thoughtful people.
> People on the outside have no idea what solitary confinement is like. The doctor shows up only when you are about to die.
> Many prisoners pair up and live as couples in the cells.
> I am fasting, so the only food you should send me is yogurt.
> My daughter makes drawings of her mother locked inside a cage.

Regarding public support for Pussy Riot:

> The jailers and judges are interested in the opinion of only one person.
> They are willing to bury us alive.

Instead of Judge Svetlana Alexandrova (who presided at the so-called Forbidden Art trial, during which curator Andrei Yerofeyev and former Sakharov Museum director Yuri Samodurov were convicted of "inciting hatred" and fined), Elena Ivanova was the presiding judge this time around.

судья Елена Иванова

JUDGE ELENA IVANOVA

TOLOKONNIKOVA: "I have a headache that doesn't go away, day or night. But they won't even give me aspirin at the pretrial detention facility."

Tolokonnikova's attorney, Mark Feygin, also pointed out several times that she had been plagued by severe headaches in jail, and should be examined by a doctor.

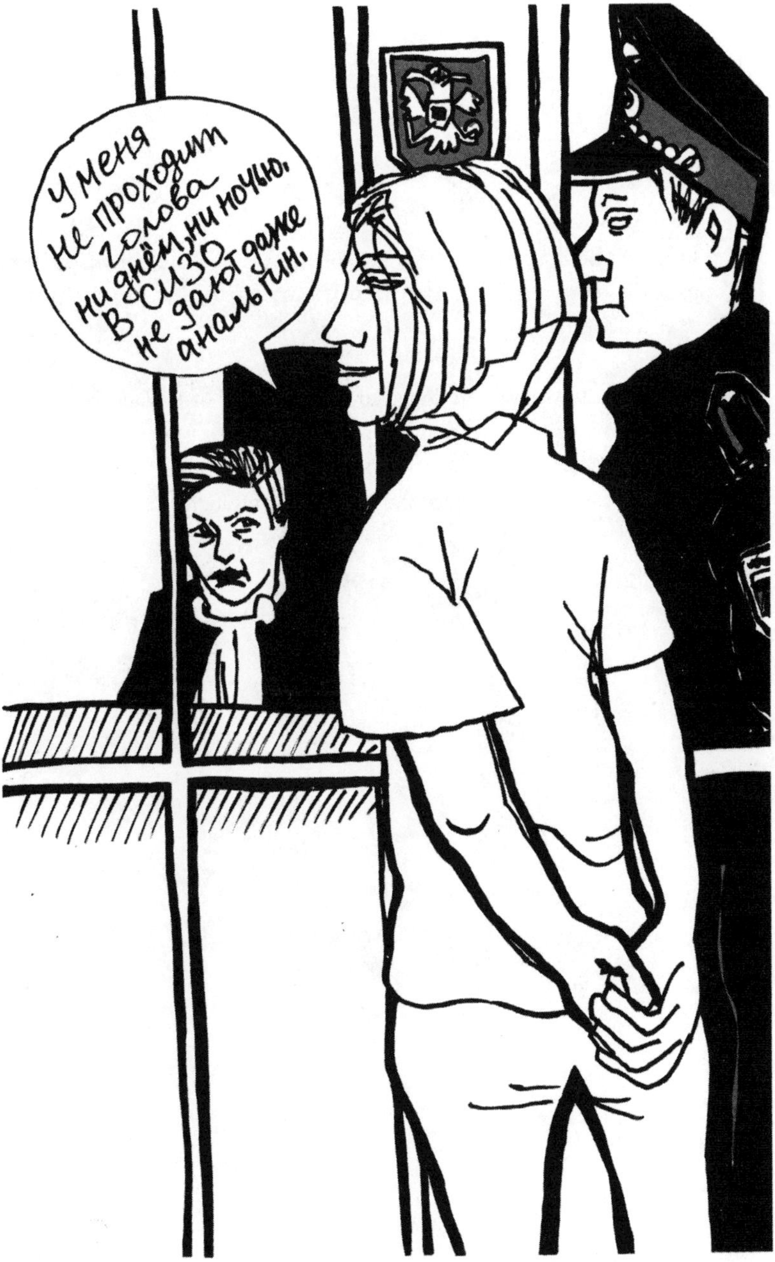
У меня не проходит голова ни днём, ни ночью. В СИЗО не дают даже анальгин.

Judge Ivanova read out the court's ruling. The police investigator's motion to extend Tolokonnikova's arrest for two months was granted.

JUDGE IVANOVA: "Tolokonnikova committed a particularly egregious crime motivated by religious hatred . . . Tolokonnikova can receive appropriate medical treatment at the pretrial detention facility . . . A young child is not sufficient grounds to turn down the investigation's motion."

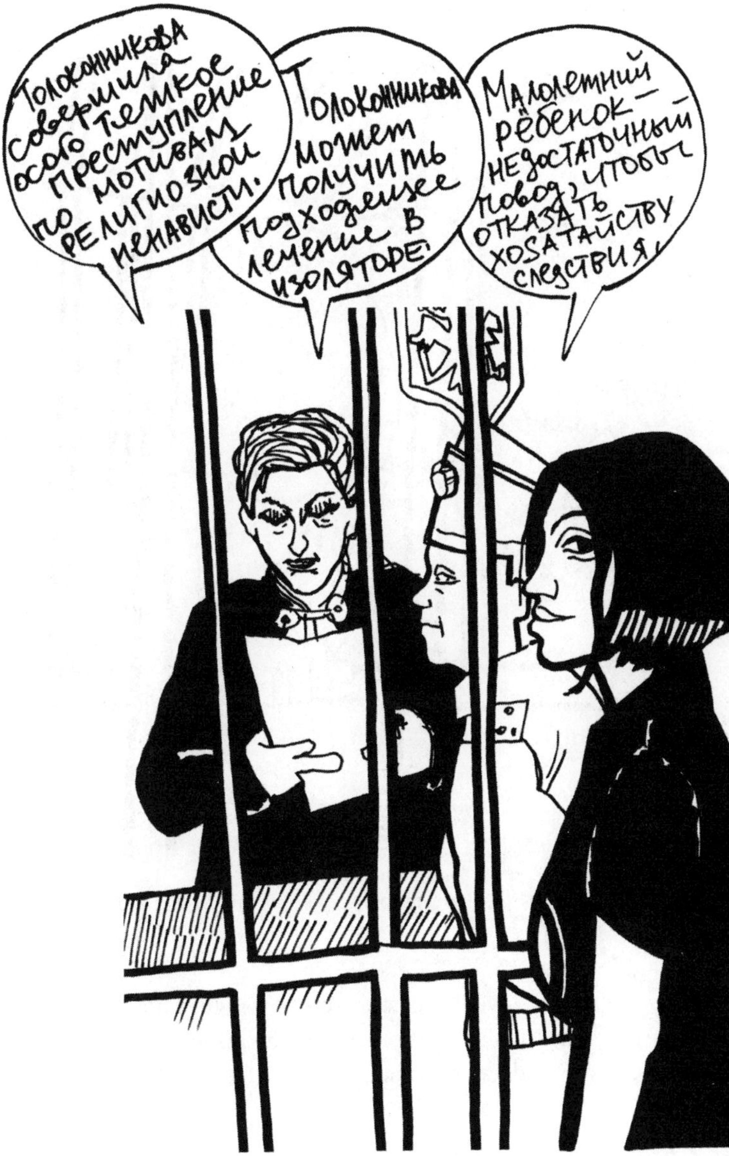
Толоконникова совершила особо тяжкое преступление по мотивам религиозной ненависти.
Толоконникова может получить подходящее лечение в изоляторе.
Малолетний рёбенок — недостаточный повод, чтобы отказать ходатайству следствия.

After Tolokonnikova's hearing, Masha Alyokhina was led in by the guards. She was carrying a book by Osip Mandelstam.

ALYOKHINA: "No, I have no complaints about my living conditions in prison."

When asked by loved ones and the press what life was like for her in prison, Alyokhina replied that she played ping-pong, read Solzhenitsyn, and had become friends with her cellmate.

Alyokhina's lawyers, Violetta Volkova and Nikolai Polozov, noted that Alyokhina was active in the community. She had worked with environmental organizations, had been involved in saving architectural landmarks, and had given drawing lessons to children in orphanages and psychiatric hospitals as a volunteer with the Orthodox youth organization Danilovtsy.

POLICE INVESTIGATOR ARTYOM RANCHENKOV: "The Orthodox community demands harsh punishment."

The positive character references made no impression on police investigator Artyom Ranchenkov.

Alyokhina smiled helplessly as she listened to the police investigator's testimony.

ALYOKHINA: "While I've been in prison, I've received around fifty letters from Orthodox believers expressing their sympathy and support."

Ranchenkov claimed there had been other letters—for example, a letter sent to the prosecutor's office by a man named Ambrosian, who believed that Pussy Riot's protests could destroy the country.

Judge Ivanova extended Alyokhina's arrest until June 24. When reporters asked her to comment on the ruling, Alyokhina quoted Mandelstam.

—Ну что ж, я извиняюсь, Но в глубине никуть не изменяюсь.

ALYOKHINA: "All right then, I apologize, / But I haven't changed a bit deep down inside."

In an interview with the Interfax news agency published the same day, Archpriest Vsevolod Chaplin, a high-ranking Russian Orthodox Church official, commented on Alyokhina's statement:

Unless they are hypocritical, apologizing and repenting do entail changing at least a little bit. I hope this step won't be the last step or the only one. I hope that the persons under investigation sense the pain they have caused and stop insisting on the "rightness" of their action in the cathedral.

Katya Samutsevich's case was the last to be heard.

> SAMUTSEVICH: "I don't give interviews about our case. One needs to be careful with names."

Samutsevich's statement to the press was the shortest. The accused said only that the trial was "political."

When she heard the court's ruling, a female police officer got the handcuffs ready.

FEMALE POLICE OFFICER: "Put your hands through here."

When members of the press left the courtroom at eight in the evening, there were still people protesting in support of Pussy Riot outside the court building. Eyewitnesses said that while the hearing was under way, police officers had aggressively detained many of those who had come to support the young women. To applause and shouts of "Set them free!" Tolokonnikova, Alyokhina, and Samutsevich were transported back to the pretrial detention facility.

THE PUSSY RIOT TRIAL

In November 2011, thousands of Russian Orthodox believers stood in kilometers-long lines in sub-zero temperatures to see a relic purported to be the belt of the Virgin Mary. The venue was Moscow's Christ the Savior Cathedral, where Pussy Riot would perform its punk prayer on February 21, 2012.

NADYA TOLOKONNIKOVA: "The Belt of the Virgin Mary can be no substitute for protest rallies."

TOLOKONNIKOVA: "I want to know why there is such a marked contrast between the two forensic examinations."

TOLOKONNIKOVA: "Is it possible that the forensic report was written using surrealist technique?"

JUDGE MARINA SIROVA: "Where is defense attorney Polozov?"

DEFENSE ATTORNEY MARK FEYGIN: "He's attempting to escort the defense witnesses you barred from entering."

PROSECUTOR: "The prosecution asks that all the defense's witnesses be dismissed."

DEFENSE ATTORNEY VIOLETTA VOLKOVA: "It's not clear why the song's claims of links between the Church and the KGB have been labeled false."

MASHA ALYOKHINA: "Who was the politician about whom I said extremely negative things?"

DEFENSE WITNESS OLGA VINOGRADOVA, ALYOKHINA'S FORMER CLASSMATE: "Vladimir Putin."

THE PROSECUTION: "Are we going spend another night in the courtroom? Think about the accused: they need to sleep."

AT RIGHT: AN ALLEGED "VICTIM" OF PUSSY RIOT'S
PERFORMANCE

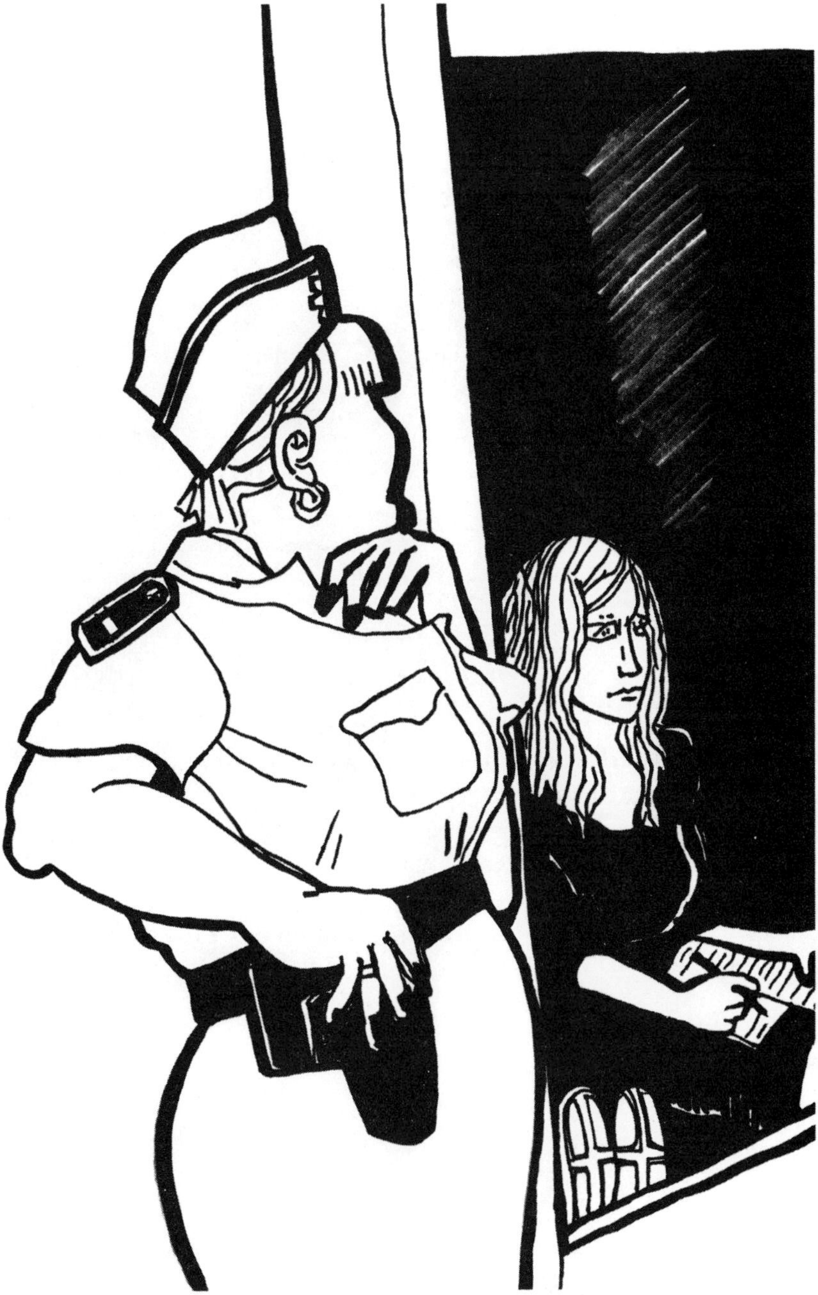

TOLOKONNIKOVA, ALYOKHINA, AND SAMUTSEVICH: "We want to go to the bathroom!"

JUDGE MARINA SIROVA: "You can go some other time."

AT LEFT: PYOTR VERZILOV, TOLOKONNIKOVA'S HUSBAND

JUDGE MARINA SIROVA: "The accused have complained that they don't like playing the role of hostages in the courtroom."

GRAPHIC REPORTAGE FROM POLITICAL SHOW TRIALS, 2013–2014

The entire world knows about the Pussy Riot trial. Artwork, drawings, videos, and documentary films about the trial have been in high demand, including my own drawings.

Unfortunately, in Russia itself, the general public is almost totally uninterested in the recent political trials and savage state persecution of such lesser known activists and grassroots protesters as Taisiya Osipova, Mikhail Beketov, and Sergei Mokhnatkin.

SIGNS (FROM LEFT TO RIGHT):
THE POLICE ARE WITH THE PEOPLE. THE PIGS ARE WITH PUTIN
SHOVE OFF, PUTIN!
FREE MOKHNATKIN!

In late February 2014, eight defendants in the so-called Bolotnaya Square case were convicted by a Moscow court of "rioting" and "assaulting police officers" during the authorized opposition march in central Moscow on May 6, 2012, the day before President Putin's re-inauguration.

SERGEI MOKHNATKIN: "I plead guilty to the fact that after all the times I have been beaten by the police, I'm still alive."

The authorities claimed the protesters had engaged in "organized mass riots." But I was there that day and I saw police savagely beating people who made no attempt to defend themselves. Many opposition activists and independent observers are convinced that the alleged rioting was actually a police provocation aimed at demoralizing the opposition and punishing those who tried to "spoil" Putin's second coronation by publicly protesting it. There are numerous photos, videos, and eyewitness testimonies that support this version of events.

TESTIMONY OF TAISIYA OSIPOVA: "My telephone was bugged. It was clear from my telephone conversations with my husband that we knew about the planned provocation against me. But I did not expect that Center 'E' officers would resort to planting narcotics on me."

The so-called prisoners of May 6 (Sergei Krivov, Alexei Polikhovich, Artyom Savyolov, Denis Lutskevich, Andrei Barabanov, Stepan Zimin, Yaroslav Belousov, and Alexandra Dukhanina-Naumova) were selected seemingly at random from the tens of thousands of their fellow citizens who were also at Bolotnaya that day. They played the role of "rioters" in the show trial that followed. They have been handed heavy sentences of up to four years in prison. Another defendant in the same case, Mikhail Kosenko, was committed to indefinite internment in a psychiatric hospital in October 2013 for his alleged crimes.

I did all these drawings with an isograph drawing pen and sketch pad in the courtroom during the trials themselves.

Mikhail Beketov, a journalist who was badly crippled after a 2008 attack in retaliation for his reporting, was brought to court in an ambulance to be tried for libel.

MIKHAIL KOSENKO, BOLOTNAYA SQUARE TRIAL DEFENDANT

JUDGE LUDMILA MOSKALENKO: "Kosenko has been accused of audacious crimes."

MIKHAIL KOSENKO: "Can I file an appeal?"
JUDGE LUDMILA MOSKALENKO: "You can do anything."

PROSECUTION WITNESS FROM THE INTERIOR MINISTRY:
"27 helmets, 29 rubber truncheons, 14 bulletproof vests, 7 shields, 3 belts,
19 gas masks, 2 megaphones, and 8 walkie-talkies were lost."

KOSENKO DEFENSE ATTORNEY: "Kosenko's mental state is unknown to the court."

DEFENSE ATTORNEYS: "At this rate, they could keep you in the pretrial detention facility for three years."

DEFENSE ATTORNEY DMITRY AIVAZYAN: "Kosenko will be in the same condition ten years from now. He has no condition that requires treatment."

PSYCHIATRIST INNA USHAKOVA, EXPERT WITNESS: "Kosenko exhibited lethargy, flaccidity, mood swings, and fear of people wanting to harm him . . ."

MIKHAIL KOSENKO: "The hardest thing is the haloperidol. It causes muscle spasms and pain."

PROSECUTOR: "Kosenko is a danger to himself and others."

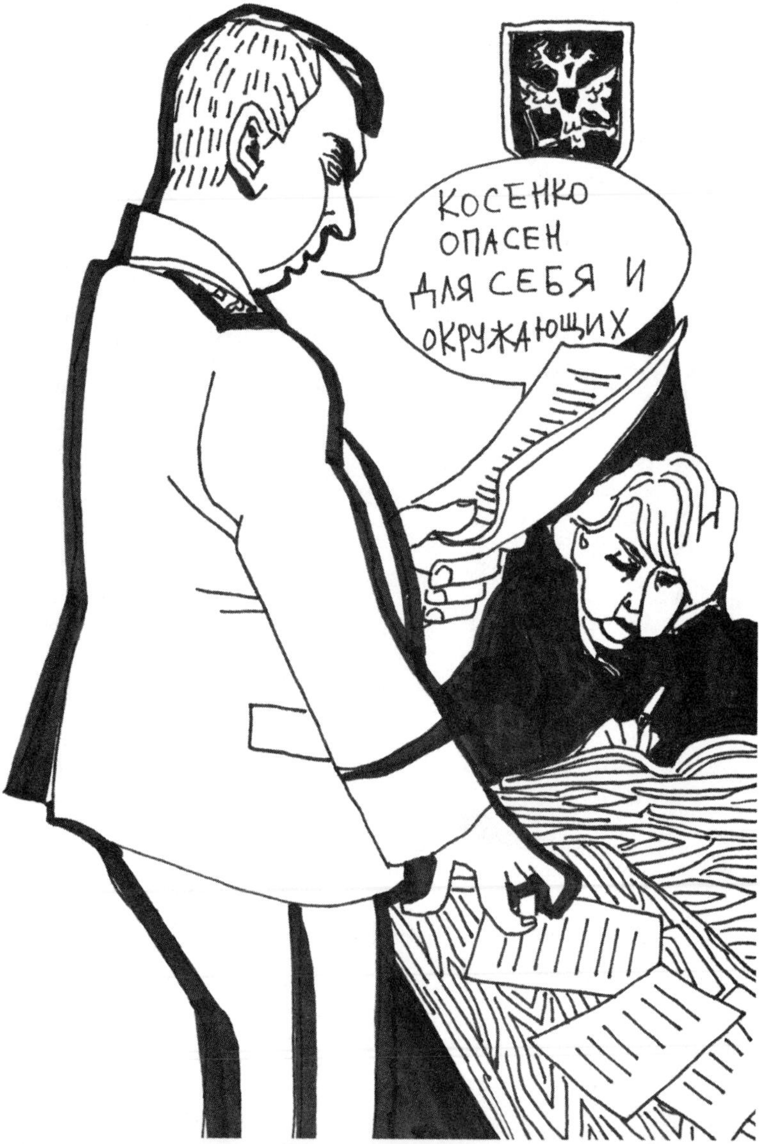
КОСЕНКО
ОПАСЕН
ДЛЯ СЕБЯ И
ОКРУЖАЮЩИХ

SERGEI KRIVOV, DURING ORAL ARGUMENTS IN THE BOLOTNAYA
SQUARE TRIAL: "I saw people with bloodied faces and battered skulls.
Police dragged a woman by her hair and beat people in the sewage that had
spilled out from overturned portable toilets."

SERGEI KRIVOV (READING FROM A POLICE REPORT DURING ORAL ARGUMENTS): "A police officer struck Krivov over the head with a truncheon, but Krivov turned away."

On February 24, 2014, Sergei Krivov was sentenced to four years in prison for "involvement in rioting" and "assaulting police officers."

ALEXEI POLIKHOVICH AND TANYA POLIKHOVICH

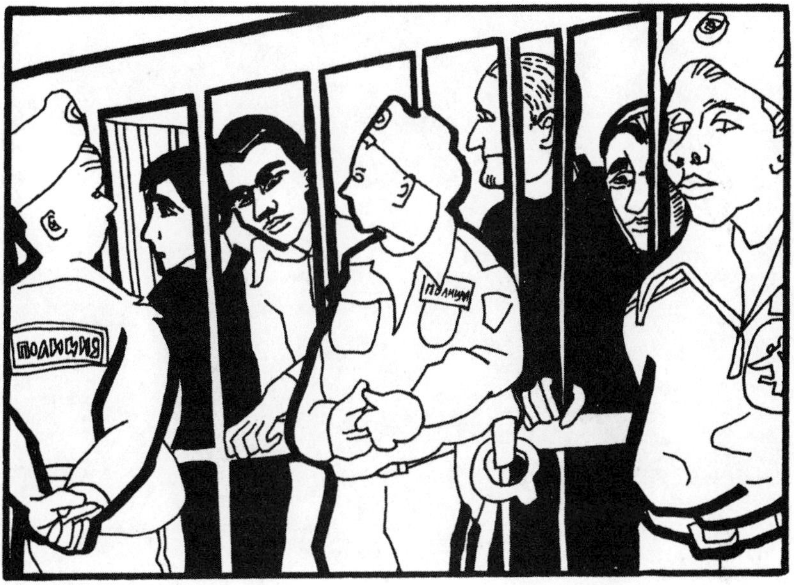
ПОЛИЦИЯ
ПОЛИЦИЯ

SIDE BY SIDE: HOMOSEXUALS AND HOMOPHOBES

When the organizers of the Side by Side LGBT film festival in St. Petersburg invited me to serve on the festival jury, I agreed right away. It was the year that gay propaganda laws were passed, and LGBT issues had taken center stage in the culture wars in Russia. I'm not an expert on cinema, and I'm not a member of the LGBT community. But given what has been happening in Russia, the festival had become a political event, and being involved in it was a clear way of expressing my civic stance.

Co-organizer Gulya Sultanova told me, "Almost all the movie theaters [the festival approached] decided to support the film festival this time, despite the potential risks. And that's worth a lot."

I found it difficult to share Gulya's optimism. I was certain that attempts would be made to disrupt the festival, and that trouble lay in store for organizers and festivalgoers.

A DANGEROUS OPENING

Police got word of a bomb threat to the movie theater several minutes before the festival's opening ceremony at the Warsaw Express shopping and entertainment complex. While police combed the building for a bomb, festivalgoers socialized outside in the chilly wind.

"There are homophobes on the corner. They're really creepy."

A gang of big skinheads gathered a few meters away from us. As Gulya later explained, these were nationalists from an organization called Soprotivlenie (Resistance). One female moviegoer standing next to me was visibly nervous.

"Now they'll start throwing rocks at us, like during the [LGBT] rally at the Field of Mars. Now they're going to fire air guns at us!"

Among the gay activists was Dmitry Chizhevsky, with a black bandage on his face. He had recently been attacked at an LGBT community center where he'd been shot in the eye with an air gun.

Side by Side organizers asked festivalgoers not to wander off by themselves.

НА УГЛУ
СТОЯТ
ГОМОФОБЫ.
ОЧЕНЬ
СТРЁМНЫЕ..

We were finally ushered into the movie theater. *Matterhorn*, a Dutch film about a father who has kicked his gay son out of the house, opened the festival.

Police escorted Side by Side viewers from the movie theater to the subway.

POST-SCREENING DISCUSSION OF *OUT IN EAST BERLIN*: "I think the tough times are still ahead of you."

"We were afraid of pogroms—that they would try and kill homosexuals in the street."

At the last minute, many foreign guests had been too frightened to come to Russia.

"We've received another bomb threat, friends!"

On five separate ocassions, the police received false threats that bombs had been planted at Side by Side festival venues. Loft Project ETAGI Art Center and Jam Hall Cinema were each threatened once, and the Skorokhod cultural center, twice.

The police and an ambulance came each time, and everyone was evacuated from the buildings where the alleged bombs had been planted. At ETAGI, the staff, hostel guests, and the patrons of its cafés, bars, and shops were kicked out onto the street along with LGBT activists.

The people responsible for the false bomb threats were never found.

SIDE BY SIDE CO-ORGANIZER MANNY DE GUERRE: "No venue will ever work with us again."

Manny's worries were justified. After the bomb threats, both the Zona Deistviya co-working space at ETAGI and Jam Hall Cinema terminated their agreements with Side by Side for the remaining screenings.

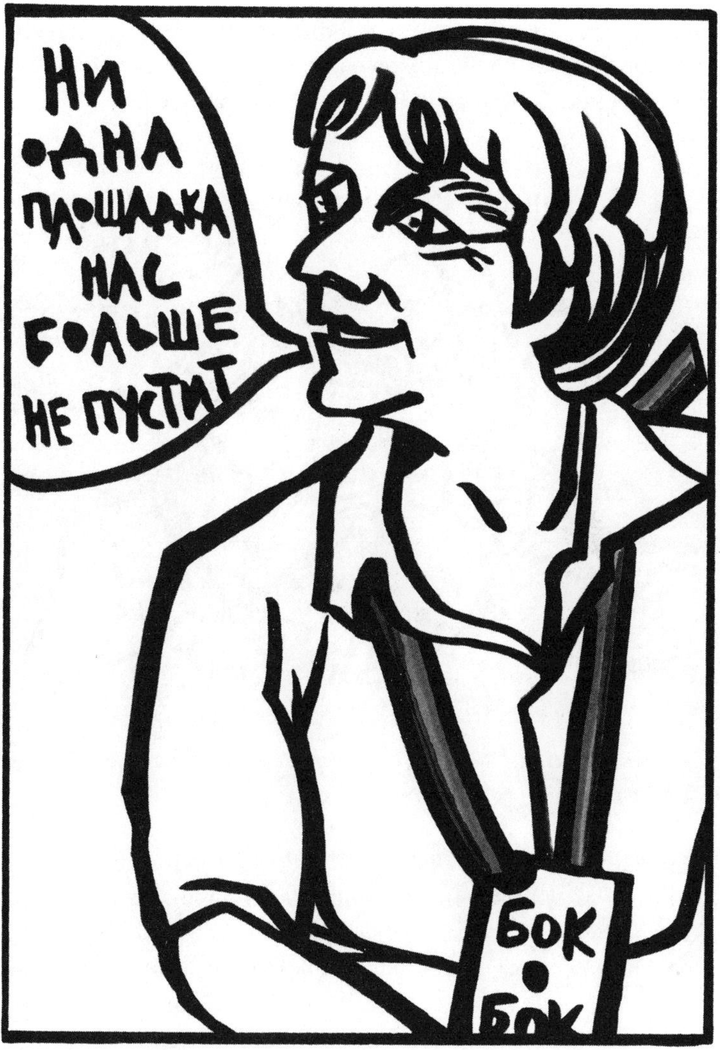
НИ ОДНА ПЛОЩАДКА НАС БОЛЬШЕ НЕ ПУСТИТ
БОК • БОК

One day, the festival program was disrupted entirely. No screenings were held, and a discussion entitled "Young People's Freedom to Access Information on LGBT Issues" was canceled.

LENA KLIMOVA: "In our city, many people don't even know the word LGBT."

Lena Klimova, a journalist and founder of the internet project Children 404, an online community for LGBT teenagers on Facebook and VKontakte, was supposed to take part in the discussion. She had traveled hundreds of miles for the festival.

The screening, at Jam Hall Cinema, of *Blue Is the Warmest Color* (*La Vie d'Adèle*), then playing without incident at many other theaters in St. Petersburg, was also interrupted by a bomb threat. The police led viewers out of the theater through the back entrance. At the main entrance, St. Petersburg legislative assembly deputy and United Russia member Vitaly Milonov demanded that police free the children whom the "sodomites" were, allegedly, "forcibly holding" at the screening. Around twenty thugs came out to support Milonov.

While waiting for the theater to be checked for bombs, Side by Side viewers took refuge in a nearby café, but several people, including me, lingered on the street. A policeman came up to me.

"Tell your people not to stand in the street, but to hide in the café. They could be attacked."

"They don't want to go into the café."

"It's dangerous, although they look like ordinary people. Maybe they won't be noticed, and no one will bother them."

What the policeman said jarred me, but it didn't surprise me. What surprised me was the absence of support for Side by Side from St. Petersburg's civic and leftist activists.

"We caught several minors in the movie theater and photographed them with their IDs."

IN THE BOMB SHELTER

After Jam Hall pulled out of its agreement with Side by Side, the festival moved to the Green Lantern Press Club, a small basement space. No bomb threats were made to this venue.

As festival jury member Bard Yden remarked, "What bombs? We're already in a bomb shelter."

The feature films *Tom at the Farm* and *In the Name Of* were shown in the "bomb shelter," along with the documentary film *We Were Here.*

In the Name Of is about a priest's struggle with his homosexual desires. Andrei, a pastor at a Protestant church, took part in the post-screening discussion.

PASTOR ANDREI: "A persecuted minority is being oppressed in the name of the church."

"I'm offended by the idea that a person can't be both Christian and LGBT."

The pastor recounted how he had once invited LGBT Christians to celebrate Easter at his church, but the other parishioners had refused to eat at the same table with them.

PASTOR ANDREI: "The Bible unequivocally treats homosexuality as a sin."

We Were Here, about the AIDS epidemic among gays in San Francisco in the 1980s, made a huge impression on me. The epidemic claimed over 15,000 lives during this period.

The US government considered introducing a compulsory quarantine, clothes with identifying marks, or special tattoos for people infected with HIV. Mass protests by the LGBT community put a stop to such plans. Gays demanded information about the new disease, the development and free distribution of medications to treat it, and government support for HIV-positive people. At the same time, the LGBT community established charitable organizations: hundreds of gay activists became volunteers, while many lesbians donated blood and worked as nurses.

One of the people featured in the film, AIDS activist Ed Wolf, came to the festival.

ED WOLF: "I've driven around Petersburg. You have many gays here. I saw them myself."

MODERATOR: "So the American government wasn't willing to solve the problem?"

ED WOLF: "An army of activists forced the government to act."

Thanks to the civic engagement of the LGBT community and, later, society at large, the epidemic in San Francisco was stopped relatively quickly.

Ed Wolf continues to work on HIV/AIDS issues. According to him, women are now at risk.

"It's hard for women to force their husbands to wear a condom every time."

Wolf also said that gays were men, too, and that it was time for them to reconsider their patriarchal views of women.

At Side by Side, I noticed that the LGBT community was not free of sexism, either. Spotting my jury member badge, one young gay man asked me what movies I would be voting for. Hearing that I had chosen *Blue Is the Warmest Color* and *Lesbiana: A Parallel Revolution*, he said, "Those films are so boring. And lesbian sex is disgusting to watch."

Most of the films shown at Side by Side were shot by male directors
and dealt with gay love. *Lesbiana* was the only feature film at the
festival made by women about women. The screening room was
half-empty: the men did not attend.

Lesbiana combines interviews with aged lesbian activists who were involved in the LGBT and feminist movements during the 1970s with documentary footage from the period. In those years there were a lot of separatist lesbian communities, where women lived and engaged in painting, sculpture, literature, music, and performance.

SHARING OUR IMPRESSIONS OF *LESBIANA* AT A CAFÉ: "I wonder whether there are 'feminine lands' in Russia where only lesbians live."

JURY DELIBERATIONS

The members of the Side by Side jury were Alexander Markov, a filmmaker; Marina Staudenmann, director of the Tour de Film international festival agency; Bard Yden, director of the Oslo Gay and Lesbian Film Festival; and two people far removed from the professional cinema world, Elena Kostyuchenko, a journalist and LGBT activist, and me.

ALEXANDER MARKOV AND ELENA KOSTYUCHENKO

KOSTYUCHENKO: "As the only LGBT activist on the jury, I'm responsible for authenticity."

Our discussion quickly shifted from the films to Russia's homophobic policies.

KOSTYUCHENKO AND MARINA STAUDENMANN
KOSTYUCHENKO: "If they start removing children from LGBT [families], our lives will change forever."

We were nearly unanimous in our choice of the winning feature film.

STAUDENMANN: *"La Vie d'Adèle."*
YDEN: *"La Vie d'Adèle."*
MARKOV: *"La Vie d'Adèle."*

Valentine Road, about the murder of a gender-nonconforming schoolboy by his classmate, won the prize for best feature-length documentary film.

THE CLOSING CEREMONY

Aside from the by now routine bomb threats, viewers who came to the closing ceremony had a surprise in store from the Rodina (Motherland) party. Party activists handed out "gift bags."

> "The bags contained rope and bars of soap, along with a note reading, 'From Russians with love.'"

GUS VAN SANT: "The people who wanted to shut the festival down caused the LGBT community to close ranks."

Gus Van Sant, the festival's most anticipated guest of honor, showed up at the Side by Side closing ceremonies with the artist Sergei "Afrika" Bugayev, whom he introduced to the audience as his "good Russian friend."

A woman in the audience asked the famed director, "What is an authorized representative of Putin's reelection campaign doing at an LGBT film festival?"

Van Sant chose not to answer the question.

AFTER-PARTY AT THE MALEVICH LGBT CLUB

Sitting among gays and lesbians at a private LBGT club, I mulled over my impressions of the festival. I had felt frightened several times during the clashes with homophobes, and I felt glad to be heterosexual. I would not be forced to live my entire life in a constant state of anxiety.

Toward the end of the festival, Gulya Sultanova said, "We're just a festival, but it feels like we're running a military operation."

LGBT activists are just people. Why must they live as if they were invisible or criminals?

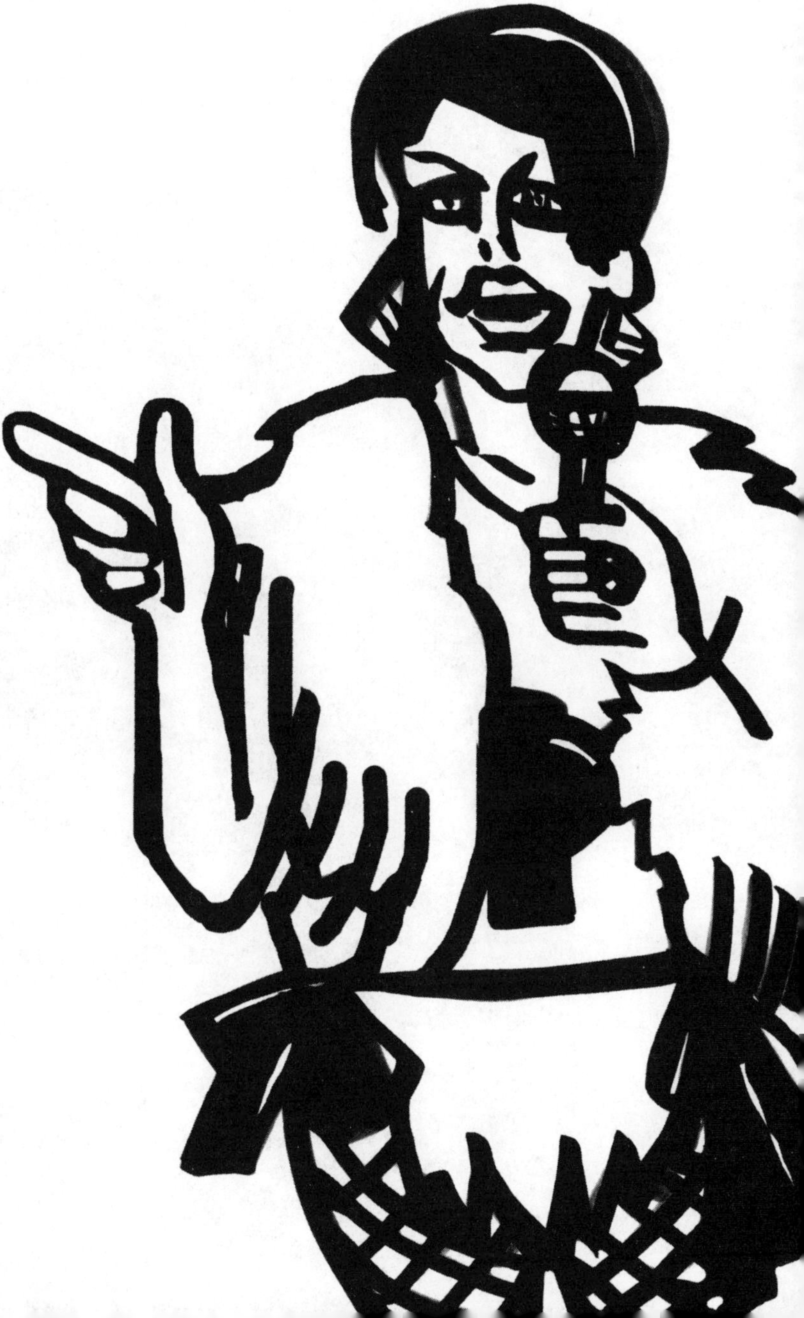

TRUCKERS, TORFYANKA, AND DUBKI: GRASSROOTS PROTESTS IN RUSSIA, 2015–2016

In late February 2015, politician Boris Nemtsov, a leader of the Russian opposition, was gunned down near the Kremlin.

Grassroots activists immediately set up a people's memorial made up of bouquets, photos, drawings, and candles at the scene of the crime, on Bolshoi Moskvoretsky Bridge. For over a year, they have been taking shifts guarding the memorial from members of various nationalist movements and bridge maintenance workers, who routinely haul away the flowers and photos as if they were trash.

ON MAN'S T-SHIRT: *NAVALNY DIDN'T STEAL THE TIMBER*,
May 24, 2016

"The assaults on the memorial occur like pogroms in a Jewish shtetl: it's the luck of the draw," these two people on vigil at the memorial told me. "They pick a time when the people on duty have let down their guard, like three or four in the morning."

"People will take to the barricades only when food runs out in the stores."

SIGN: *THE 'RUSSIAN WORLD' HAS NO USE FOR SCIENCE AND EDUCATION*, June 6, 2015

Headed by opposition leaders and attended by thousands of people, the 2012 rallies and marches for fair elections and a "Russia without Putin!" ended with the show trials of 2013 and 2014 against opposition leaders and rank-and-file protesters.

Over the last couple of years, the Marches of Millions have given way to small-scale rallies and protests. People far removed from politics have tried to defend their own concrete rights.

I made these drawings at a rally in defense of the Dynasty Foundation. An NGO founded to support scientific research and science education in Russia, Dynasty had been declared a "foreign agent" by the Justice Ministry.

"Today, they killed Nemtsov. Tomorrow, they'll kill a nationalist leader."

TORFYANKA

In June 2015, residents of Moscow's Losiny Ostrov (Moose Island) District came together to stop construction of a church in their local park, Torfyanka. The building had been planned as part of the Russian Orthodox Church's 200 Churches Program.

"People need hospitals and kindergartens more than they need another church on the site of our park." Torfyanka Park, July 1, 2015

Residents set up a tent camp in the park and stood watch in shifts to keep construction equipment from entering the site. They also filed a lawsuit, asking the court to declare the public impact hearing on the construction project null and void. The hearing had been held without their involvement.

"I have two kids, but no dacha. We're always here at the park in the morning and in the evening. We need the park." Torfyanka Park, July 1, 2015

As I was drawing the people defending the park, nearly all of them made a point of saying they were interested only in saving Torfyanka, not in politics per se.

The Russian Orthodox Church and city officials were not expecting a fight. It is seen as something of a miracle when people in Russia engage in successful grassroots organizing. "Cossacks," veterans of the military conflict in the self-declared Donetsk People's Republic, and members of the Russian Orthodox grassroots movement Multitude arrived at the proposed building site, which had been fenced off.

AN ORTHODOX VOLUNTEER, SPEAKING TO OPPONENTS OF THE PLANNED CHURCH: "I don't even know what is going to happen to you. The fifth column has already shown up here." Torfyanka Park, July 1, 2015

After the outbreak of hostilities in Ukraine, Russian TV and pro-Putin newspapers frightened their viewers and readers on a daily basis with stories of "national traitors" and a "fifth column." People who attended anti-war rallies, for example, were identified as part of the fifth column. Any protest against the regime was likened to a "fascist Maidan."

— Я боюсь, что если такой Майдан, как на Торфянке, начнётся везде, как бы мне не закончить эмигранткой в какой-нибудь скучной Франции.

Плачевна судьба людей, которые не смогли навести порядок на родине...

The park's defenders claimed that only a handful of neighborhood residents supported building the church.

"We are also Orthodox and are in favor of building a church, but not in our park. Churches should not be like bakeries. There doesn't need to be one on every corner," they explained.

They also said that people were going house to house and scaring pensioners by telling them they would go to hell when they died if they opposed construction of the church.

THE CAMP AT KHIMKI

Russian long-haul truckers undertook the most notable protest campaign of 2016.

In November 2015, the Russian government introduced new regulations for calculating tolls paid by cargo haulers traveling on federal highways. A special system for paying the tolls, called Platon (Russian for Plato) was set up.

According to truck owners and drivers, Platon would collect 400,000 rubles annually from each truck. That would be tantamount to bankruptcy for them. The first fine for not paying the toll had been set at 450,000 rubles, and fines for each subsequent failure to pay were set at one million rubles. Fifty percent of the company running the Platon toll system is owned by Igor Rotenberg, son of Arkady Rotenberg, a billionaire from Putin's inner circle.

In late November and early December 2015, truck drivers from several Russian regions set off for Moscow in their rigs. Police stopped the drivers on the outskirts of the capital and made them turn their empty trucks around, but approximately twenty-five drivers managed to break through the blockade and set up a camp in Khimki, twenty kilometers outside of Moscow.

On December 4, 2015, the Russian government reduced the fines for nonpayment of tolls in the Platon system by 98.9%.

I first traveled to the truckers' camp in Khimki before the New Year. It was the weekend, and people continually drove up to support the protesters. They mainly brought food and diesel fuel. The truckers were grateful, but they looked wary.

"In the early days, we pushed everyone away and were suspicious of each other. We didn't know each other then," trucker Sergei Vladimirov, a coordinator at the camp, would say a month later.

I drew a portrait of Andrei Bazhutin, a trucker from St. Petersburg who would soon emerge as a leader of the protesters. I could sense he was at a loss.

"We're having a strike here, while five meters away people are getting ready for New Year's."

Decked out with signs bearing protest slogans, the trucks looked out of place next to Khimki's huge shopping centers and crowds of people doing their holiday shopping

ANDREI: "After the New Year, everyone will come to their senses, but the truckers in Khimki will be gone. We need support now."
SIGNS ON TRUCK: *NO TO PLATON* and *I OPPOSE TOLL ROADS*, December 26, 2015

I met Dmitry, one of the defenders of Torfyanka Park, at the Khimki camp. He was heartened by what was happening.

DMITRY: "The authorities are putting too much pressure on people. We have an idea to link this protest up with the one in Torfyanka."

SIGN: *WE WANT TO FEED THE WIFE AND KIDS, NOT OLIGARCHS*

December 26, 2015

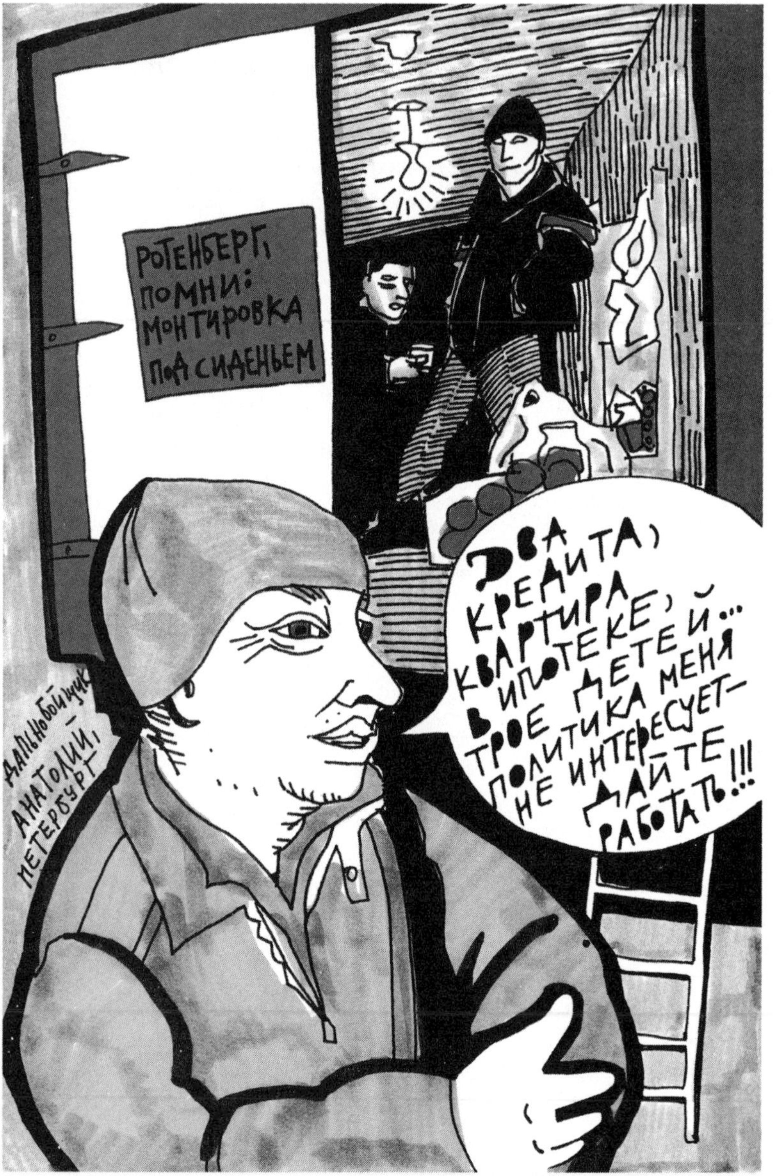
РОТЕНБЕРГ, ПОМНИ: МОНТИРОВКА ПОД СИДЕНЬЕМ
ДВА КРЕДИТА, КВАРТИРА В ИПОТЕКЕ, ТРОЕ ДЕТЕЙ... ПОЛИТИКА МЕНЯ НЕ ИНТЕРЕСУЕТ — ДАЙТЕ РАБОТАТЬ!!!
ДАЛЬНОБОЙЩИК — АНАТОЛИЙ, ПЕТЕРБУРГ

At that point, though, the truckers themselves just wanted Putin to pay attention to their campaign and abolish Platon so they could go back to their ordinary lives.

> ANATOLY, A TRUCKER FROM PETERSBURG: "I have two loans, the apartment is mortgaged, and three kids. I am not interested in politics: let me work!!!"
> SIGN ON BACK OF TRUCK: *REMEMBER, ROTENBERG: THE TIRE IRON IS UNDER THE SEAT*, December 26, 2015

"We are not involved in politics," the truckers would tell everyone who visited the camp.

One of them put it this way: "You have to have the knack of politics to make political demands."

Meanwhile, on social media, leftists and liberals were discussing whether to support the truckers. Many of them were disappointed the truckers were not organizing a revolution.

I happened upon Tamara Eidelman, a prominent member of the liberal intelligentsia and an award-winning schoolteacher, at the Khimki camp. She was giving a lecture on nonviolent civil resistance. (She had lectured on the same topic during Occupy Abay in 2012.)

TAMARA: "My acquaintances tried to scare me by saying the truckers were zombies."
MAN: "They don't even know us."

Eidelman wrote about her trip to meet the truckers in a blog post on the Echo of Moscow radio station's website.

"I looked around and could see they really were interested. I saw I was surrounded not by ferocious wild men, but by attentive listeners with intelligent faces."

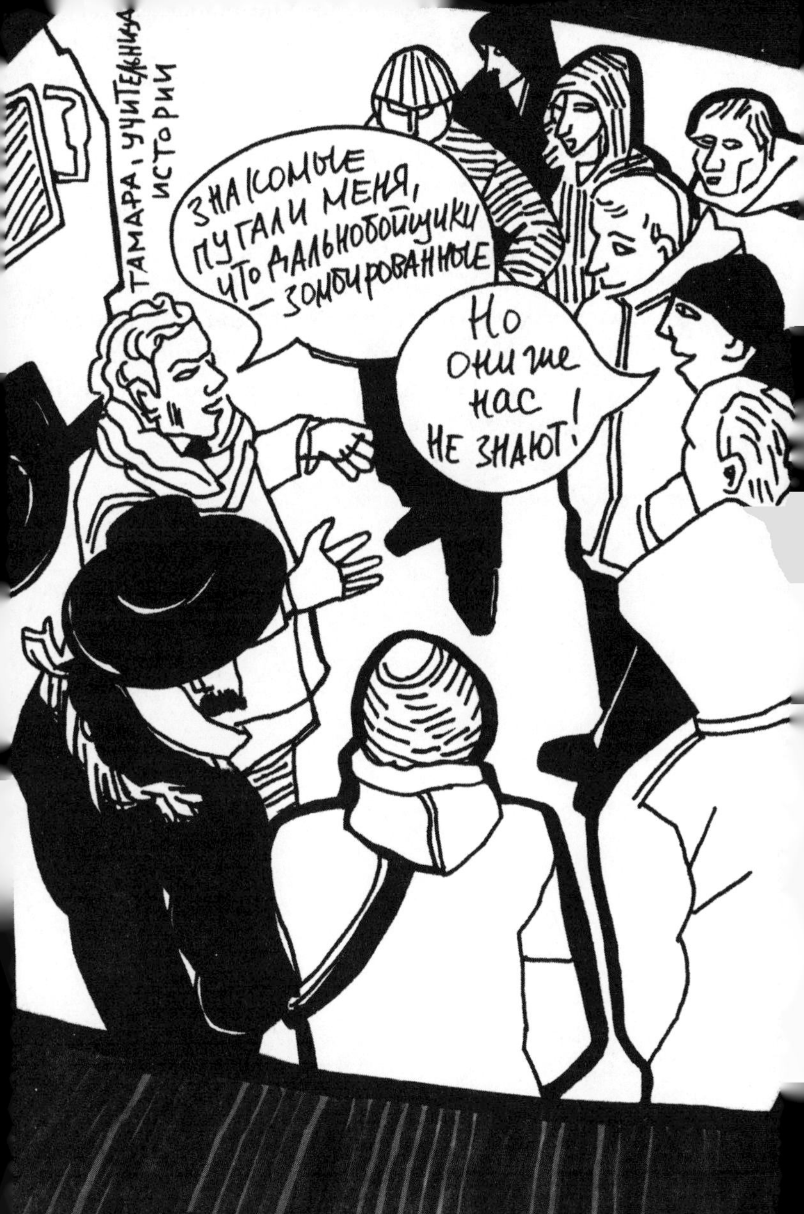
ТАМАРА, УЧИТЕЛЬНИЦА ИСТОРИИ
ЗНАКОМЫЕ ПУГАЛИ МЕНЯ, ЧТО ДАЛЬНОБОЙЩИКИ — ЗОМБИРОВАННЫЕ
Но они же нас НЕ ЗНАЮТ!

This is a portrait of Tasya Nikitenko, press secretary for the truckers. A 20-year-old student at the Institute of Journalism and Literature, she had come to the Khimki camp at her own behest and lived there for a couple of months, helping the protesters communicate with the press.

"At first, I expected the striking truckers to park their rigs on Red Square."

The liberal media (RBC, Novaya Gazeta, Meduza, TV Rain, and Colta) regularly covered events in the camp. But the campaign was virtually invisible on national television, and Prime Minister Dmitry Medvedev dubbed the strikers "mediocre truckers" who "haul who knows what." This caused the truckers to lose faith in Russian television and turn to online news sites.

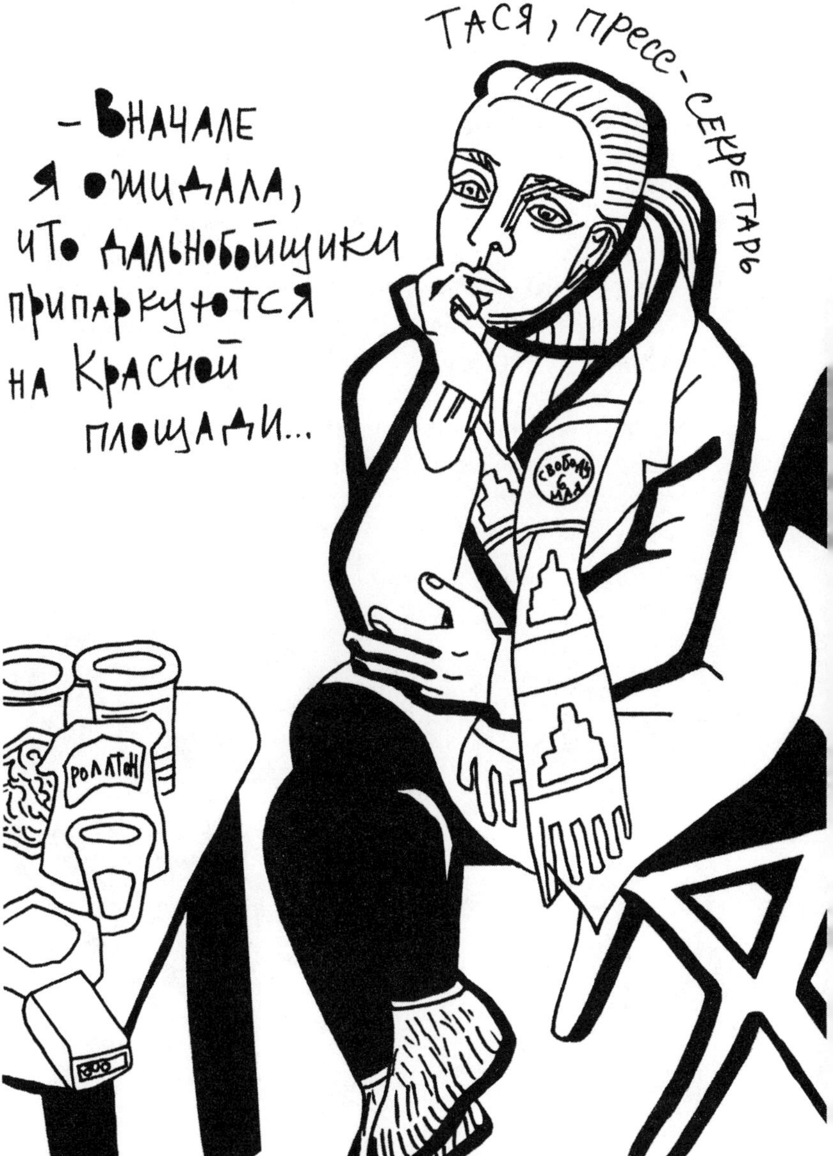
Тася, пресс-секретарь
— Вначале я ожидала, что дальнобойщики припаркуются на Красной площади...
свободу 6 мая
РОЛЛТОН

THE CAMP AFTER THE NEW YEAR

After the New Year, the truckers set up a headquarters in one of the semitrailers, which they equipped with a table, stools, a gas stove, and shelves for porridge and potatoes. Guests would stop by the headquarters, and nearly all of them tried to help out in some way. Ivan, an economist who lives nearby in Khimki, regularly brought the truckers hot meals he cooked himself.

"My contribution is minimal," said Ivan. "After I started coming here I began sleeping better."

ALEXEI, A VEGAN TRUCKER, AN ACTIVIST, AND IVAN, AN ECONOMIST FROM KHIMKI: "When the Kremlin clock chimed, we listened to a video address by truckers instead of the president's address."

Ivan rang in the New Year at the Khimki camp. Activist Pavel Pechnik and his comrades organized a celebration for the truckers.

"There was a large table laden with homemade food. There was a freshly cut fir tree," Ivan told me. "I expected it would be good, but it was grand. I felt like these strangers were my relatives."

Ivan gave the truckers eleven copies of Plato's dialogues, because "they dialogue about Plato here every evening."

The winter days were cold and dark. The truckers and their visitors sat in the headquarters in stocking caps, jackets, and fur coats, warming themselves with tea served in plastic cups and debating philosophy, history, veganism, environmentalism, and politics.

A young entrepreneur visited the camp several times and gave the truckers money for diesel fuel. The camp survived on donations (an account was opened at the State Savings Bank), but many campers still had to go into debt or sell their trucks to survive.

"If they outmuscle all of you, they'll slip their hands in everyone else's pockets." January 10, 2016

Elena, a reporter, provided a daily account of events at the camp on a Facebook group page entitled "Coordination of Truckers: No to Platon!" Tatyana, a singer, held concerts at the headquarters, and the truckers could go to her house to bathe and wash their clothes whenever they wanted. Katya, a lawyer, helped out by giving them money and legal advice.

Truckers arrived from other cities to see the camp firsthand. Two truckers from Kursk were impressed.

"In Russia, people always look up to the big cities. We are going to tell our people back home, 'Boys, the whole country is rising!'"

CAMP VISITORS, January 23, 2016

Anatoly, a trucker from Khanty-Mansiysk, recounted how truckers in his region had tried to fight back against the Platon toll system.

"We gathered in Surgut for a protest. A helicopter was flying overhead. Then the riot cops dispersed us. Nothing else happened after that."

"If I couldn't change anything at home, I had to go to Moscow," Anatoly decided.

He had arrived by car with his friend Sergei, a trucker from Chelyabinsk.

"The police will use any excuse to keep us from making it here in our trucks. They break the law and confiscate our licenses."

Andrei Bazhutin told visitors how life in the camp had been changing.

"In the early days, chaos reigned, but the guys are like soldiers now. We have figured out what 'newsworthy' means and how to give interviews, but the demand on us has been such that it feels like we've been doing this for years."

"The camp is a like a lighthouse. It has to be here." January 10, 2016

Dissatisfied with the existing Interregional Trade Union of Professional Drivers, the truckers had originally wanted to set up a new trade union. That proved impossible, because many of the protesters were workers and employers at the same time. They decided to establish an association of carriers instead. All the decisions were made at closed-door meetings.

ANATOLY: "Thanks to Platon and Rotenberg we are now founding a real alliance." January 10, 2016

Andrei, a trucker from Togliatti, brought over a hundred people to the meeting.

"Because our town is in ruins," he explained, "All that is left of industry there are two chemical plants, and they are on their last legs."

Over fifty drivers and truck owners from Shenkursk, a town of 5,000 people, joined the alliance.

"Trucking is the main occupation in our town. There is nothing else to do," said Kirill, from Shenkursk.

The largest truckers' strikes took place in Dagestan. In November 2015, when the protests against Platon kicked off, Dagestani drivers also headed for Moscow. Truckers from Russia's southern regions stopped at the ninety-first kilometer mark on the Kashira Highway. Dubbed the southern camp, it lasted for over three weeks.

During one of my trips to the Khimki camp, I met Rustam Mallamagomedov, interim representative of the Dagestan Union of Truckers.

"After a meeting involving all of Dagestan's districts, at which we elected our own representatives, the police visited all of them at home."
February 2, 2016

A few weeks later, Rustam would accidentally find out he was on the police's wanted list, charged with organizing an "unauthorized rally."

Приехал я сюда
не от хорошей жизни,
понял — всё будет
ухудшаться,
Мой маленький
грузовичок
пропустили.

Сергей, Дагестан, Хасаюрт

"Ordinary people support us," Sergei, another trucker from Dagestan, told me. "They realize that if haulage costs go up, produce will cost more. Bananas are imported to Dagestan from Iran. They cost 23 rubles a kilo, but after the new regulations were adopted, they went up to 29 or 30 rubles a kilo."

> "I would have not come here if it had been up to me. I realized things would only get worse. The police let my tiny truck through." January 23, 2016

I met him again during my next trip to the Khimki camp. He was grim.

"My boss is selling the truck tomorrow. The business has become unprofitable. The internet is awash with trucks for sale."

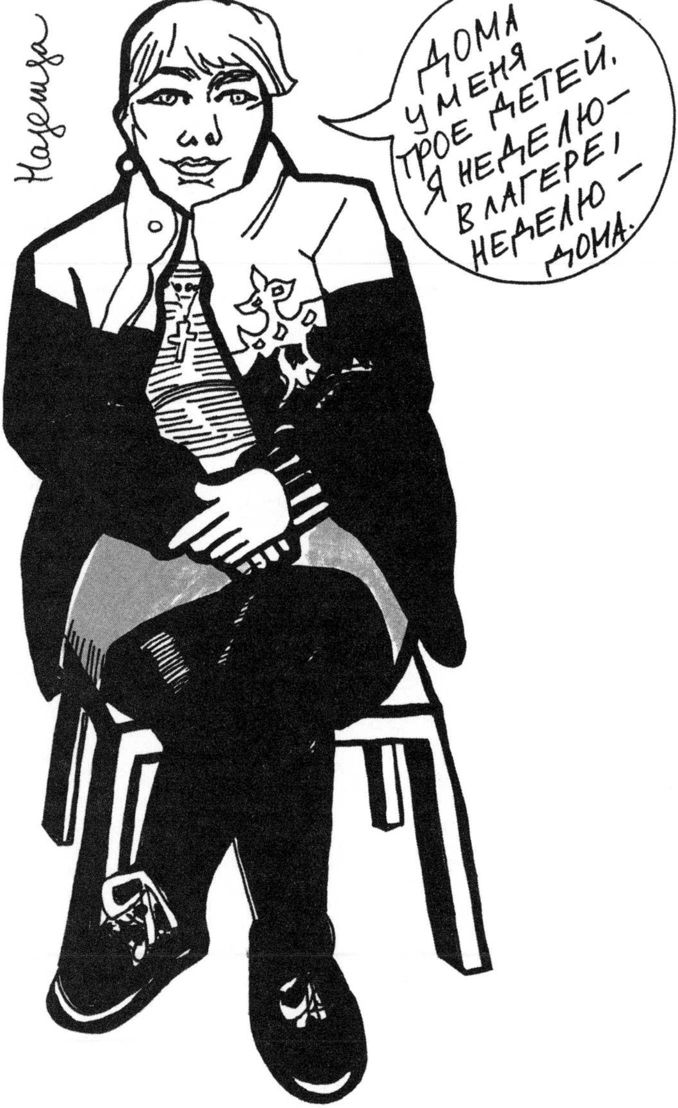
Надежда
Дома у меня трое детей. Я неделю — в лагере, неделю — дома.

The only woman at the camp was Nadezhda, from the Vologda region. She used to work as a manager in the housing authority, but left "because the whole business is dishonest." She owned two trucks. She had been at the camp since day one.

> "I have three kids at home. I spend a week at the camp and a week at home." February 2, 2016

"I'm grateful to Platon for helping me meet such a variety of people here," said Nadezhda.

—

Carriers have many other problems besides Platon. Intermediaries are one of the biggest. This was how the truckers described the situation:

> The "stools" (dispatchers) man the phones. They manage several trucks, so companies find it easier to contract with them. We truckers couldn't agree on the haulage rates among ourselves. The bids are organized among dispatchers. If they don't have trucks available, they pass the job on, and they take a cut of the fee every time they do this. From the late '90s until the '00s, the stools charged between 5 and 7 percent, but nowadays no one knows how much they are charging.

Many truckers are certain dispatchers take cuts of 50 to 80 percent.

Unsafe roads are another problem.

"The protection rackets have made a comeback. Rigs are getting broken into again, like in the '90s. I try to make stops only at paid parking lots or places that are tried and true," said Oleg, a trucker.

Truckers who worked in the Far East talked about how they would ford frozen rivers and lakes, their doors open and their passports in their pockets. There are many sinkers—submerged vehicles—on the bottoms of these rivers and lakes.

THE STRIKE

On March 1, 2016, the toll for a kilometer of cargo truck travel on federal highways was supposed to rise from 1 ruble and 53 kopecks to 3 rubles and 6 kopecks. The activists at the Khimki camp decided it was not enough to keep the camp running and hold meetings in the regions, so they organized a nationwide truckers' strike.

The protesters were convinced toll roads for trucks were only the beginning. The tolls would destroy the existing cargo transport system, leaving it in the hands of monopolists.

"The days the big rigs stop running: February 20 to . . ." February 9, 2016

I made a poster for the strike. The cities identified on it were places where truckers had held rallies, meetings, and strikes.

TRUCKER, YOU'RE NOT ALONE! NATIONWIDE STRIKE,
FEBRUARY 20–MARCH 1, 2016

NADYA, ALEXEI, AND MIKHAIL

ALEXEI: "Yesterday, we leafleted the truck stops. Many truckers didn't know about the camp in Khimki." February 2, 2016

Truckers rarely use the internet, and the protests were not covered on TV. Most of the drivers who talked to campaigners at truck stops supported the activists at the Khimki camp.

The truckers wrote a three-point list of demands:

1. Abolish the Platon toll system and punish those responsible for it.
2. Abolish fees for major repairs in apartment buildings and institute a two-year moratorium on increases in utility rates.
3. Reinstate discounted travel for pensioners and disabled people in all regions.

"These are basic demands, because they affect everyone. Everyone gets old, and everyone has parents," the truckers explained.

"We've been able to convince many truckers to join the strike. There is nothing to lose now, and it is too late to worry." February 9, 2016

HE FED ROTENBERG HIS FILL,
AND PAID OFF PLATO:
MEANING, HE BENT OVER DOGGIE STYLE
AND OPENED HIS ASSHOLE!

Before the strike, the Khimki camp activists held meetings in several cities where they shared their self-organizational know-how.

"In the regions, they want to see the truckers from Khimki, because they trust us," said the activists. But they didn't have the money to keep making these trips.

—

I was not in Russia during the strike. When I got back, I went straight to the Khimki camp to hear the news. Trucker Mikhail Kurbatov summed up the strike's main outcome.

МIKHAIL: "The government has frozen the rates. We have not formed an alliance yet, but we have done this for the country."

The toll rate per kilometer remained unchanged.

According to the activists at the Khimki camp, between fifty and sixty regions were involved in the strike. Ninety percent of drivers in Dagestan went on strike, forcing supermarkets to prepare in advance for it. Truckers set up temporary protest camps in St. Petersburg, Nizhny Novgorod, Vologda, Tyumen, Khakassia, and Orenburg. A new temporary camp also sprang up in Tyoply Stan, on the outskirts of Moscow.

Most TV channels totally ignored the strike.

ANATOLY AND ALEXEI. ALEXEI: "Killing a man in Red Square is a brazen thing to do." March 21, 2016

Maxim, a trucker from the Khimki camp, went to the new camp in St. Petersburg for two days.

"They have as many trucks as we have. Most of the people were from St. Petersburg. There were truckers flying the slogan 'Down with the government.' Then they left, and the regular guys stayed."

There were ninety people in the new truckers' alliance before the strike, but around 300 afterwards.

The truckers also took part in the memorial march for opposition leader Boris Nemtsov.

"When they said we were a 'fifth column,' we realized how easy it was throw mud at anyone."

TORFYANKA AFTER THE NEW YEAR

After talking with several defenders of Torfyanka, the truckers went to visit their camp. They realized they would need to unite to change things in Russia.

DARYA, AN ACTIVIST: "The truckers brought us oranges and canned meat. We have been supporting each other on a personal level."
February 6, 2016

The battle for the park had been going on for eight months. The residents proved that the public impact hearing had been fictitious, and the authorities did not extend the developers' permits to do excavation work on the church building site.

"They have been allocated another lot, but it cannot be expanded. They were planning a sports complex for Multitude and a house for ministers here," said Darya. "The new site is in a more heavily populated area, but the locals would never attend church here after so many travails."

Darya also talked about an assault by men from Multitude and the inaction of the police.

"I'm a believer, but now I've stopped going to church. I won't baptize my children: they can decide for themselves. And of course I will tell them the story of Torfyanka Park," Darya said.

—

The residents on duty at Torfyanka invited me into their tent. It was a cold day, and my hands and feet were numb after twenty minutes. During the winter, the watches lasted three hours. People kept themselves warm with blankets and hot tea. An activist whom everyone called Aunt Valya would bring trays of pancakes and pies to the people on watch.

"We used to be estranged from each other, but now we're friends. We socialize and visit each other at home. We're involved with our neighborhood. We got the roads improved and new elevators installed. We even got the stairwells painted," the local activists said.

They also talked about their attempt to march onto Red Square in T-shirts emblazoned with the slogan "Movement for Torfyanka Park." Ten people took part in the protest. The police detained all of them, and each was fined 10,000 rubles.

"We rang in the New Year here. There were a lot of people in the tent."
February 6, 2016

The residents said that, initially, they had a ban on talking about politics in the camp. "But, unfortunately, we seem to have been involved in politics for a while now," they said with a sigh.

Multitude continued to hold prayer meetings at Torfyanka in support of building the church. Composer Andrei Kormukhin, a leader of the organization, spoke at one of the meetings.

ANDREI KORMUKHIN: "People who support Maidan and Radio Svoboda were here. They were counted as local residents for some reason."
SIGN AT LEFT: *BUILD THE CHURCH!*
SIGN ABOVE KORMUKHIN: *THE MORE CHURCHES, THE FEWER GAYS*
MULTITUDE RALLY, TORFYANKA PARK, February 6, 2016.

He also asked people to pray for the Orthodox activist Lyudmila, who had vandalized several works by the famous sculptor Vadim Sidur at the Manezh, Moscow's central exhibition hall. She had been sentenced to house arrest.

"No crackdowns on the Orthodox!" shouted Kormukhin.

—

I heard the following conversation between a married couple during the religious procession.

"What if we make the sign of the cross at them [the pro-Torfyanka activists]?"

"We already did. And we whacked them upside the head. It didn't work."

MULTITUDE RALLY, February 6, 2016

On February 13, 2016, Multitude was scheduled to hold another rally. But the night before, members of the organization attacked the tent where local residents were on watch. The Torfyanka activists telephoned the truckers, who immediately came to their aid.

TRUCKERS: "We got a call from Torfyanka in the middle of the night. They said, 'They're beating up the girls!' When we arrived, the police were already here." February 13, 2016

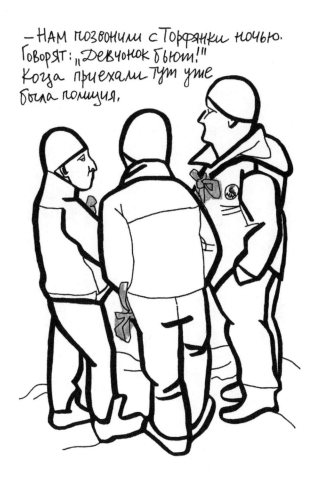

— НАМ ПОЗВОНИЛИ с ТОРФЯНКИ НОЧЬЮ.
Говорят: „ДЕВЧОНОК бьют!"
Когда приехали тут уже
была полиция,

Darya recounted what happened.

"Around fifty men in masks cordoned off the entire area. They wanted to deliver logs to the construction site on the sly, under cover of night. The police just stood and watched until someone from Multitude threw a log at the police. Then about twenty-five of the Multitude guys were detained."

—

Multitude went ahead with their rally that afternoon. Enraged by the nighttime assault, a large crowd of area residents also gathered in the park. They blew whistles and sang the Internationale, drowning out the speeches and prayers at Multitude's rally. The police formed a human chain and set up fences to separate those attending the rally from the locals.

WOMEN: "Get the hell out of the park!"
STRIKING TRUCK DRIVERS: "The authorities have gotten pretty brazen, and the Church is doing their bidding."

On their page on VKontakte, a popular social network, Multitude described the confrontation as follows:

Everyone who attended the rally today came face-to-face with the gaping maw of Maidan and the Devil's whistle. Rushing to the scene at the beck and call of their leaders, activists from the wormy Yabloko Party, PARNAS, the "truckers," and their ilk decked the local gang of ecclesiaclasts in the green ribbons of their organization and stuck a whistle in each of their mouths!

DUBKI

In March 2016, in addition to the clashes at Torfyanka, conflict flared up at another Moscow park. Residents of the Timiryazev District opposed construction of a huge twenty-two-story residential building with an underground parking lot on the edge of Dubki Park. Developers planned to build the high-rise on the site of a former kindergarten and an avenue of oaks.

On March 26, locals held a rally to save Dubki Park. Children's drawings from a competition entitled "I Love Dubki" were hung on the park fence. Many people came with their children (many of whom were the competing artists) and enjoyed perusing the drawings before the speeches began. Recordings of "The Grasshopper Sat in the Grass" and other Soviet tunes played over a loudspeaker. I heard old women reminiscing.

"There used to be little houses here, and a grove where there were nightingales."

Several activists from Torfyanka and the defenders of Friendship Park (where a stadium has been under construction) came to support the campaign. Mikhail Barbotkin, a Friendship Park defender, said it was dangerous if there were too few men on the night vigils at threatened parks, because private security guards were used to doing their dirty work at night.

After the rally, I quizzed Mikhail about the defense of Friendship Park. He recounted serious clashes between private security guards and residents in which both sides had suffered injuries.

MIKHAIL: "For the time being we are holding on like Leningrad during the Siege, but the state has more resources and can wait us out."
SIGN: *FRIENDSHIP PARK AND THE DEFENSE OF THE LEFT BANK DISTRICT SUPPORT DUBKI!*

Sergei Mitrokhin, a leader of the Yabloko Party, and members of several other political parties spoke at the rally. Residents reacted sluggishly to them. But they applauded when an activist from the Save Dubki pressure group said, "We don't need politics. We have a concrete issue!"

SIGN: *BRING THE OAKS BACK TO THE PARK!*
INSCRIPTION ON BACK OF T-SHIRT: *LET'S SAVE DUBKI*

After the rally, I met Dmitry, one of the people who stood watch along the fence erected by the developers. At the outset of the campaign, the activists stood watch in the daytime, going home at night. One morning, however, the locals looked out their windows and the trees were gone. The developers had chopped down the avenue of oaks overnight.

"When the private security guards were here, it was as scary as being in a war."

As I drew him, Dmitry talked about his parents, who had lived on the street, in the Ivanovo barracks, and about his grandfather, who had left from here to go to the front.

"My history is here, and they want to take it away."

When the conflict was over, Dmitry was sure his know-how as an activist would be huge. After victory in Dubki, he would be able to help defenders of other parks.

"I should also say thanks to the developers for acquainting me with so many wonderful neighbors," he concluded.

At the spot where Dmitry and several other activists were keeping vigil, I met two very tiny watchmen. Albert and Nargiza, brother and sister, lived in the neighboring district. They had come to walk in their favorite park and accidentally happened upon the rally. Albert had read about the defense of Dubki online, and the children decided to join the vigil.

"I called Mom, and she gave us her approval," said Albert.

ALBERT: "I go to the school across the street from the park, and I hang out in the park with friends."
NARGIZA: "Dubki Park makes children and squirrels happy."
INSCRIPTION ON NARGIZA'S VEST: *FRIEND OF DUBKI PARK*

On March 31, 2016, the locals were unable to stop construction vehicles from entering the site. Several of the residents were injured in a clash with security guards. Some of them were taken to the hospital, while around fifteen activists were detained and taken to a police precinct.

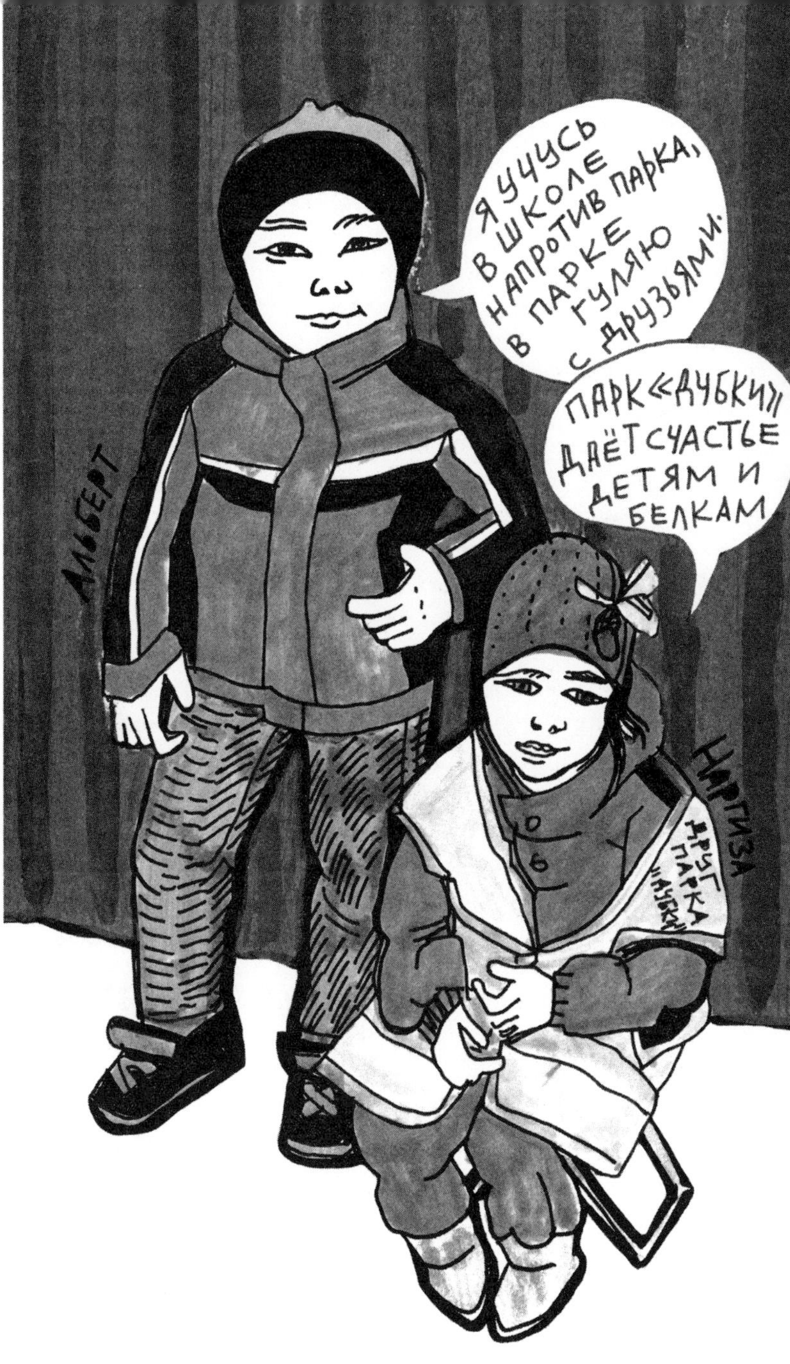
Я учусь в школе напротив парка, в парке гуляю с друзьями.
ПАРК «ДУБКИ» ДАЁТ СЧАСТЬЕ ДЕТЯМ И БЕЛКАМ
АЛЬБЕРТ
НАРГИЗА
ДРУГ ПАРКА «ДУБКИ»

UNDER PARTY FLAGS

In early April 2016, an anti-Platon rally, featuring such political parties as PARNAS, Democratic Choice, Yabloko, and the Communist Party, was announced. The Khimki activists and their allies among the regional truckers' alliances decided not to take part in the rally after voting via Skype.

There were several reasons for this. One of them was that the rally's organizers were not truckers and did not know their problems from the inside. The campaigning truckers had also decided not to march under any flags. It was crucial that ordinary people trusted them, but ordinary people no longer trusted any of the parties. Finally, it was too early for them to jump into politics before they had founded their new association.

"We have to talk not as individuals with other individuals, but as an alliance with other alliances," they said.

After starting out with the problems of truckers, nearly all the speakers quickly segued to calling for the regime's overthrow: "Down with Platon! Sack the government! Down with Putin!"

Among the speakers was Ilya Lvov, chair of the St. Petersburg branch of Democratic Choice, and Svetlana Stosha, director of a transportation company and president of the alternative Union of Carriers. Both Lvov and Stosha had periodically attacked the Khimki campers online for what they saw as a wrongheaded campaign, for "compromising with the ruling party" and "sabotage and betrayal."

ILYA LVOV: "Don't forget! Don't forgive! We'll take our revenge on election day." April 3, 2016

SEND PLATON TO THE TRASH! SACK THE GOVERNMENT!

CIVIC INITIATIVE FOR FREE MEDICINE AND EDUCATION

Alexander Kotov, head of the Interregional Trade Union of Professional Drivers, and Nikolai Matveyev, chair of the Miass local of the Union of Professional Drivers, spoke out in support of trucker Alexander Zakharov, who had been charged with murder on flimsy evidence and sentenced to nine years in a maximum security prison.

"By sentencing Zakharov, they were telling all truckers, 'Don't make waves! Do as you're told!'" April 3, 2016

At the rally, I saw Yevgeny, a trucker from Vologda, whom I had met at the Khimki camp. He told me how the strike had gone in Vologda.

"There were twenty-five trucks in the camp from February 20 to March 1. The first two days, the police chased us around in earnest and tore down our posters. Charges have been filed against the campers, and they're facing fines. During the strike, three people in Vologda were 'de-Platonized,'" meaning they had stopped using the Platon toll system.

Ten or so other truckers from Vologda had come with Yevgeny to the rally. They even rented a van for the trip to Moscow. They were clearly proud to be involved.

"You have to take advantage of every conflict. We're not ashamed of ourselves. We didn't stay home and lie in bed."

YEVGENY FROM VOLOGDA: "They are right to say, 'Down with Putin!' It was he and his cronies who dreamed up Platon."
SIGN: *VOLOGDA VS. PLATON*, April 3, 2016

The Khimki camp activists were not happy about the fact that the Vologda truckers had attended the rally. This offended the guys from Volodga.

"Politics and life are dirty. What, do you want to be squeaky clean? What difference does it make whom we unite with? What matters is that they're also opposed to Platon," argued several of the outraged Vologda truckers.

But for the Khimki campaigners, the hows, whys, and whos mattered when making alliances. Their main goal at that moment was establishing their own alliance.

"Our alliance will be like socialism within a democratic society," said Mikhail Kurbatov when describing the future association.

MIKHAIL AND RUSTAM. MIKHAIL: "Only reliable, decent people should remain in our association."

THE FOUNDING CONGRESS

On April 30, 2016, the Khimki camp activists organized and held the founding congress of the Association of Russian Carriers (OPR) at the Lenin State Farm in the Moscow region. According to their tally, approximately 300 drivers from thirty-one regions attended the congress.

A report on the Platon system listed its flaws, in particular erroneous debits, problems with registering, and the inability to use the system in areas with no internet coverage.

SIGNS ON CURTAINS: *ASSOCIATION OF RUSSIAN CARRIERS*,
April 30, 2016

"The rates for cargo trucks were calculated based on the assumption that a truck travels 8,000 kilometers annually, while actual annual mileage is between 100,000 and 150,000 kilometers," said one of the speakers.

The truckers voted unanimously to establish the OPR. Andrei Bazhutin was elected chair of the OPR by a majority vote. One representative from each region was elected to the association's council. The congress was designated the OPR's main governing body.

POSTERS ON TRUCKS: *NO TO PLATON, FOR ALEXANDER ZAKHAROV,*
AND *CARRIERS VS. UNEMPLOYMENT*, April 30, 2016

After the congress, its delegates and the activists who had supported the truckers went to the Khimki camp. The camp had never looked so festive and animated. The headquarters was too small to accommodate everyone, so they socialized outside.

—

Both joy and sadness were palpable at a small banquet late in the evening. It was clear it was time for the truckers of the Khimki camp to part company. Nearly all of them had gone heavily into debt and incurred the wrath of their wives due to their long absence.

They had wanted to take part in a May Day rally, but all three applications they made were rejected on the pretext that all the venues were taken. So the camp dispersed the day after the OPR was founded.

Dozens of activists—people who had become their friends while the camp was in operation—gathered to say farewell. The truckers of the Khimki camp departed in a single column, their rigs sporting the blue flags of the Association of Russian Carriers.

THE SUPPORT GROUP

After the truckers departed, their most loyal friends—Elena, the journalist; Ivan, the economist; and Katya, the lawyer—met to celebrate the singer Tatyana's birthday. I was also invited.

We were united by our memories of the Khimki camp, and we spent the whole evening talking about it.

Ivan cooked "protest food" for us. That was what we called the potato pancakes and red tea he would often bring to the truckers.

"I just knew you would be nostalgic about the camp," he said.

"When the camp was depressed, I would make extra-large beef cutlets to brighten the mood."

— Когда в лагере была депрессия, я делал специальные большие котлеты по поднятию настроения.

I knew Katya spent her free time volunteering at orphanages and nursing homes. She was also involved in her district's grass-roots pressure group, and was moderator of a group opposing paid parking.

"The truckers came to support a rally against paid parking where I spoke. After that, we saw each other every day."

The conversation kept returning to the question of why so few people had understood how important the events in Khimki were.

"People like being good angels to the sick and unfortunate. Most people don't understand why they should help the strong, but the strong end up pulling everyone else along with them," argued Elena.

"When you help out in an orphanage, you're helping only that orphanage. When you help the truckers, you help everyone," Katya said, agreeing with Elena.

We decided to keep helping the truckers as much as we could.

ON THE TABLE: PROTEST POTATO PANCAKES AND PROTEST TEA

ACKNOWLEDGMENTS

I would like to thank my friend, the artist and translator Bela Shayevich, whose efforts made the publication of this book possible; translator Thomas Campbell, who, for several years, has been translating my reportage as part of his political activism; everybody at *n+1*; my Russian publisher, Dmitry Yakovlev, who has been regularly showing my work in Russia; and my parents, for their boundless support.